Antony Gormley Inside Australia

Antony Gormley Inside Australia

Thames & Hudson

with 206 illustrations, 118 in colour

Y T o n A R D O G m L E

Many thanks to the Menzies community for all their support, encouragement, hospitality, humour, and brave and generous participation.
Antony Gormley

Inside Australia is a UWA Perth International Arts Festival Commission. All the Insiders are identified wherever possible. The participants in the project are listed on page 176.

First published in the United Kingdom in 2005 by Thames & Hudson Ltd, 181A High Holborn, London WC1V 7QX

www.thamesandhudson.com

British Library Cataloguing-in-Publication Data
A catalogue record for this book is available from the British Library

ISBN-13: 978-0-500-51262-3
ISBN-10: 0-500-51262-0

Design by SMITH
Printed and bound in China by C&C Offset Printing Co., Ltd.

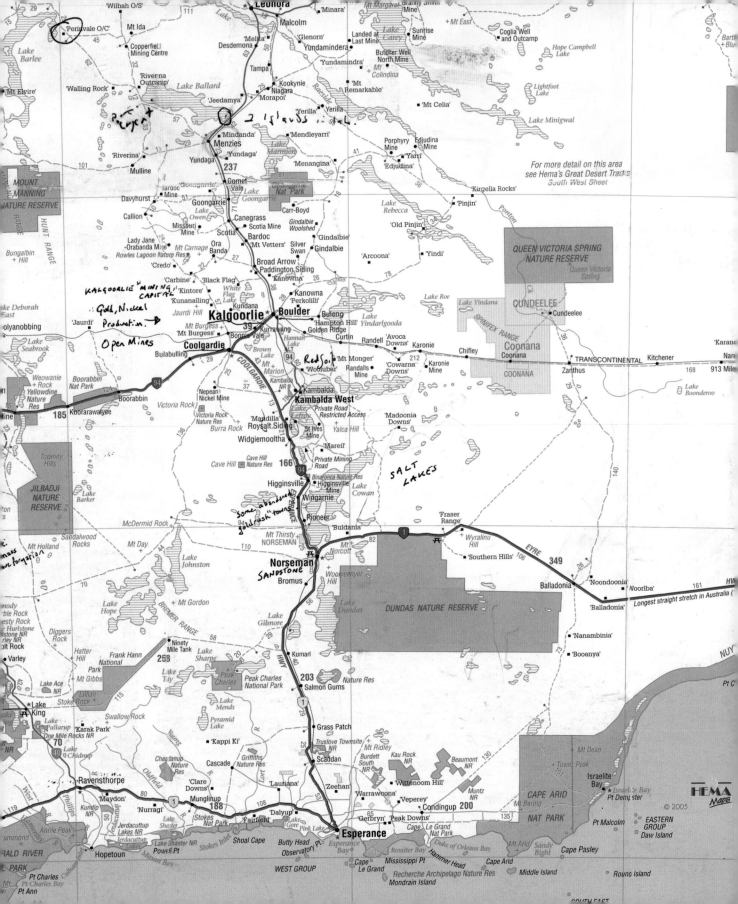

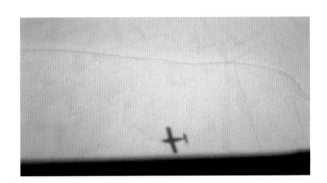

**Every place you walk, you have to have a story.
Know what is, see where you are, know where to go.**
Edward Johnston, Wangkatha, Menzies

**My father came here for the mines; I worked on mines. Been here thirty-five years,
in this little place we call our bush camp. Everything closed.**
Allan Henderson, former miner, Menzies

**Those Aboriginal corporations and mining companies, they're eating away at tradition.
No traditional knowledge, and people try things that won't work.**
Kath Finlayson, former pastoralist, Kalgoorlie

**Maybe the first thing that has to be said is that reasonable art comes from a degree
of reason, therefore you don't get good art without some form of good thinking.**
Antony Gormley, artist, Lake Ballard

Inside Lake Ballard

Hugh Brody

First steps

The first steps I took inside Australian's western desert were on the
forecourt of the Menzies' garage, cafe and petrol station. Antony
had driven us from Perth, leaving at 5am and stopping only for food
and camping supplies in Kalgoorlie. We had been hurrying to meet
with Paddy Walker, the Aboriginal elder who had to give his
permission for the *Inside Australia* project to go ahead.

There was another car on the forecourt, a ute with its doors open.
An old, very dark man with white hair and beard sat in the front;
another, younger man was leaning against the truck. On the garage
wall, I noticed a poster with pictures of different poisonous snakes
and a few lines about what to do if you were bitten. A third
Aboriginal man was leaning on the wall beside the poster,

'Hey', he called out to the others, 'This is the guys we're meeting.'
He was Ralph, he said, 'and this is Ron and', pointing to the elderly
man in the truck, 'this is Paddy Walker. He's the law man.' We shook
hands all round, apologizing for having kept them waiting. Ron said
it hadn't been for too long, but we had better get going, out to the
lake. He said they'd follow us out there. 'We can just follow your
tracks', said Ralph. 'We can follow tracks, that's why they call us
Black Fellas.' And he burst out laughing.

The wind was gusting hard from the north-west, the direction in
which we were heading. Dark clouds were piling up ahead. We drove
out on a long dirt road. After about fifty kilometres, Antony slowed
and somehow managed to find the mark that showed where we were
to turn off to Lake Ballard itself. We went along a faint track,
through the scrub, and came to a sand dune that rises to form the
lake's south-west shore.

It was an astonishing landscape: the surface of the lake dead level,
one wide arm stretched ahead, another disappearing around a
headland to the south-east. Even under the dark, gloomy sky, the lake
seemed to glow. No more than a hundred metres from the shore, a

19

Interior, abandoned Gwalia mining town

strange island rose in a perfect cone from the surface. Beyond it were other islands, low and faint as they appeared one beyond another.

A few minutes after we arrived, Paddy, Ron and Ralph drove up. They told us to go closer to the lake shore; the sand dune was firm enough to drive on. It was beginning to rain and the wind was still strong. 'Better get inside', said Ron and he got into the driver's seat, alongside Paddy. Antony and I climbed into the back seat, Ralph's considerable size causing us to squash hard against him. It was a tight fit.

Ron turned round. 'Well,' he began, 'we've been talking about this sculpture idea on the way here, and Paddy here says it's all right. He is giving you permission to go ahead.' Then he went on, 'But to do this, you have to know the story. He'll tell you the story in his words, in his language, and I'll translate for you.' He turned to Paddy. 'Right, go ahead, tell them the story, then.'

Paddy Walker told us the story in a soft voice, speaking mostly in his own Ngulutjara language, giving short pieces of the tale in cryptic form. We were hearing an outline, key bits, the essence. Ron made it clear that this was a story from the Dreamtime. As Paddy spoke, the wind blew hard enough to rock the car, and then the rain poured down, clattering on the roof and across the windscreen. We seemed to have removed ourselves from any actual place. In a strange cocoon, we listened.

'This is woman's dreaming. You are a lucky man to have found a woman's dreaming. You know the seven sisters stars? The seven sisters stars in the sky? This is on their path. They came across the lake here, playing around. They stopped here.

'That island right in front of us, the largest of the islands, that is the oldest of the sisters. The other islands, heading out there, up the lake, are the other sisters, the younger ones. Down the lake there are two hills, look like young girls' breasts. Those hills were made by the

Above: Ralph Ashwin
Opposite: Paddy Walker, Wangkatha elder

splitting of an egg-shaped stone by a boomerang. Further on is a place where one of the sisters fell down and laid on the ground. You can see the marks, where her breasts went into the ground, and where her face touched the ground.

'This is where the sisters came down from the sky and were playing around out there. Then a man began chasing them, trying to catch the youngest one. So they had to run away. They had to hide. They hid in rock holes. There are rock holes down the shore of the lake, back where we came from just now, and they hid in those seven holes. This is on the camping route to Jeedamya and Morapoi. Then they came up through the lake, and became the islands out there. One island leads to another, one after the other, way up the lake there. That's where they were heading, to this place. You have to know what you are looking at, what these places are.'

Paddy was giving us just a glimpse of the Seven Sisters, enough to know that as you walked out among these islands you would be going into their terrain. And enough to have a sense of connections — between the story and the land around us, the earth and the sky, the present and most distant past.

At one point, as the rain came down in a sudden torrent, Ron said 'This is the sisters making the rain. I guess they are not happy that we are telling you their story.' But Paddy and Ron kept going. And once Paddy had told us as much as he wanted us to hear, they talked about other things. Ron was concerned to make sure that we understood Paddy's status.

'Put it this way,' he said, 'if this was the white fella's army, this man' — pointing to Paddy — 'would be commander in chief. And this man' — pointing to Ralph — 'would be sergeant.' They all laughed.

We also talked about names. Paddy's Aboriginal name was Bajata. 'The name his mother gave him, his nickname', said Ron. Ralph's surname was Ashwin, after his white grandfather, and through

Vance Blizzard in front of Snake Hill, Lake Ballard

whom Ralph told us he had ties to many families in Europe, including one family of Ashwins in Italy. Ron explained that he had been given the name Ron Smith by the Schenks, the evangelists who ran the Mount Margaret Mission where he had been sent as a small boy. His father was a white man called Harrington, who had been on his deathbed when Ron met him. They all had many links, to the land around us, through their dreaming to many other parts of the land, and, through all parts of their heritage, to places far, far away.

The rain let up, and we got out of the car. Antony asked if there would be more rain later. 'No', said Ron. 'We've told you the story now; the sisters are feeling OK.' As we stood outside Ron's ute, he repeated that Antony had permission to work on the lake. But there had to be an agreement: everything had to be the same when it was all over as it is now. Nothing can be changed or damaged.

Later I was to hear other parts of the 'Seven Sisters Dreaming' story. I was taken to see the rock holes where the sisters hid. I was shown a little of how the line of the story reached to the north, touching the earth as rock holes and dream sites, until it reached another dreaming line going across the Seven Sisters. In one version of the story, the sisters are chased by a wild man, penis out and erect, with many ritual scars and determined to seize the youngest of the girls. In another version, I was told of a handsome young man who loved one of the sisters and wished to dance with her. And I was told about a tree at the east end of Lake Ballard that is one of the sisters, standing there, alone and waiting to join the others. The stories were many, various, complicated and, at times, confusing. But they always led from the lake, or the rock holes, in dream trails to other places. They sit as one thread in a great web of stories and knowledge.

In this way, the Dreamtime stories are like the many different groups to which each Aboriginal person belongs. You have the country you were born and raised in, the place 'you walk about' and know as your own, your 'Ngurra'. This gives you links to those who grew up there, walked about there with you. And you have your totem or sign, which comes from the father and is linked to the spiritual events of conception. This establishes bonds with others who have the same totem. And you have your 'skin', which has to be different from that of either your father or mother, but will be the same as others all over the Desert region. This means that you have family – parents, cousins, siblings and children – in many Aboriginal communities. Wherever you find people with the same 'skin', you belong – even if it is to a people and place you have never seen. So everyone belongs to very specific places, where they have lived, hunted and gathered, attended ceremonies; and everyone belongs, also, to many, many other places and peoples. Languages, Dreamtime stories, dreaming sites, names and 'skins' make up this web of connection – rooting a person in Ngurra, while allying everyone to a large, intricate Aboriginal world that spreads all through the centre of Australia.

But the Aboriginal people here hold onto the threads that lead from one part of their world to another, from this lake up into the skies with the seven stars of the Pleiades, along the surfaces of the rocks to the places they walked as children, and through the bush and the people who use and have lived there – threads that are strong and almost invisible, like the silk of spiders, attaching them to a web of people and places far away from Lake Ballard.

First Europeans

On both sides of the lake stand ridges of rubble and thin shafts into the earth: the work of gold miners. These are small pointers to the industry that brought white Australians into the region, and sustained them there.

In 1869, John Forrest, the man who would later be the first premier of Western Australia, led an expedition into the western desert. Forrest's guide and companion was Tommy Windich, an Aboriginal from another land, but able to lead Forrest along Aboriginal trails, discover water holes and help manage relations with Aboriginal groups they ran into. They spent 113 days crossing 2,000 miles. The western desert did not hold out great prospects for the new Australian frontier economy. The land seemed forbidding, disagreeable, arid and of little economic significance.

But in 1892, prospectors found gold nuggets and evidence of rich gold-bearing ore in Coolgardie and then near Kalgorla, an Aboriginal dreaming site, which the prospectors wrote as Kalgoorlie. News of the find leaked out. Within weeks a gold rush burst into Western Australia. At first the rush centred on the Coolgardie and Kalgoorlie discoveries. But in 1894, groups of prospectors began to head north, probing a line that created staging points with names

that tell us how far they had got from Coolgardie: a track led to 'Twentyfive Mile', then on to 'Ninetymile', and then some twenty miles beyond this. Two of the men who were pushing their way along this track were L. R. Menzie and J. E. McDonald. They depended on 'Jimmy', an Aboriginal who did their tracking and kept them safe in the bush; and on Cumbra, an Afghan camel driver, who kept their supplies loaded and moving. At Ninetymile, Menzie met J. J. Brown, a miner who had already sunk a shaft. Menzie was eager to purchase an existing mine for the Perth syndicate that backed him; he set out to inspect the site.

The terrain was not easy. Misreading their route, Menzie and his party ran out of water, had to take an eighteen-mile side trip to the east, and then headed back too far to the west, travelling to one side of the Brown shaft. But while they were lost, Menzie suddenly noticed nuggets and quartz that were heavy with gold. They realized that they had struck rich. Leaving Jimmy and Cumbra at the site, Menzie and McDonald set off to register a claim. On 1 October 1894, they secured two leases, which became the Lady Shelton and Florence mines. Other claims were registered. Within weeks, out in a remote corner of the Australian bush, a town was being built – or rather, thrown together. By the end of 1895, the town, given the name 'Menzies', had three hotels, a tent hospital, a post office, a town clerk, two policemen and two banks. Five years later, there were thirteen hotels, a railway line, two breweries, a school and, at its peak, a population of close to 10,000.

By then, 50,000 miners had come to the region. They created many towns not far from Menzies: Niagara, Kookynie, Malcolm and Leonora, to name a few. Each of these has its own story of sudden boom, astonishing vigour (the brewery in Kookynie, with a peak population in 1905 of 1,500, is reported to have made 400,000 gallons of beer in ten years) and real hardship (all the towns endured

29

Above: Saline deposits and dried mud on the surface of Lake Ballard
Opposite: Map showing mining and pastoral leases around Lake Ballard

drought, fierce summer heat, floods and deadly outbreaks of cholera and typhoid). The people who came to live and work in these places were brave, resourceful and, in their own world, humane.

The Lady Shenton was the most productive gold mine in the area (yielding a total of some 132,000 ounces of gold); but there were others too: Queensland Menzies, Crusoe, Friday, Florence, Aspasia-Pandora and Lady Sherry. The names of these mines — like the whole story of the gold rush to places like Menzies — say something about the culture of the newcomers. Or at least their distance from the cultures that were alive in the country into which they had ventured and laid claim. There are few if any names with Aboriginal origins; and there were few if any links between the miners and the Aboriginal people they met. It is true that the first explorers and prospectors depended on Aboriginal trackers and guides — for the most part, men who came from other regions. But once camps had been set up, roads and railways opened, and Menzies was in place, Aboriginals were of no use to the community or the industry. They were not looked to as labourers. Even the freight system before the railways came depended on Afghans and their camels rather than on Aboriginal strength or knowledge. The photographs and documents from the time, like the histories that recall the great explosion of the gold frontier in Western Australia, pay scant attention to the Aboriginal people who occupied the Goldfields before they were seen as fields of gold.

At a tough frontier, where men came with a grim determination to live a rough, hard-drinking life in order to get rich beyond dreams, societies grew that were touched, and perhaps made bearable, by every kind of effort both to meet and to soften hardship, loneliness and ill-health. A collection of writings and memories from Kookynie includes the poignant couplet:

Rubble at an open cut gold mine near Kalgoorlie

Little deeds with pleasant meanings,
Hungry hearts can understand.

That kindly deeds did not include any real effort to respect or make an accommodation with the Aboriginal people stands as no special judgment on the mining frontier: an activity of its times, it shared with the rest of Australia a sense of utter estrangement from Aboriginal heritage. What existed as society was what white people created — however sudden or improvised or alien. And what miners created was indeed sudden and alien — bursting onto the most arid and rugged of lands with a need for services, progress and water.

Mining is about only one kind of relationship to the land where it takes place: extraction of that which brings wealth. There is no need to nourish the earth to ensure that ore exists, or increases. Nor is there an inclination to widen the project to other kinds of wealth: when it comes to gold, the miner focuses his all on the way to find the wealth that would mean he could go and live in luxury elsewhere. And once the chance for this wealth has gone, so too is everyone and everything else that the mining frontier brings with it. The land, along with other ways of using, knowing and living in it, is found, mined and then left to fend for itself. There is drama to the gold frontier: the booms are sudden, extreme, exciting. Thousands of people rush to one place, then to another; communities spring up in the unlikeliest places; great shafts and holes are smashed into the earth, while millions of tons of rock are crushed and searched for the particles of wealth they are believed to conceal.

Standing at the lake or in Menzies, thinking about miners and mining, the rest of the world seems far away. But all frontiers come from somewhere else, and lead back there. The people who poured into the area, and created the Menzies boom, travelled from many parts of the world. Men who had suffered disappointment in the

31

California goldfields; men who had come from Europe to find new kinds of freedom in Australia; men who had drifted across Australia, drawn by the latest mining book. And some women: a few wives at first, more later, and then families with children born into the new towns. Prostitutes, too, of course – at its peak, Kalgoorlie had a whole street of brothels. Society came from elsewhere: the languages spoken were those of other places, other countries, as were the books and magazines people read and the syle of clothing they wore – especially for the big occasions. The newcomers brought with them their horses, dogs, cats, and the germs of the diseases from which they suffered. As the money came, so the things money bought came as well. Almost everything was imported, from water to building materials to basic foodstuffs. The economics of the market – of relative values, the costs of imports and exports to the region – shaped life at every level. Consortiums in New York, London, Wales and the cities of Australia determined what happened in places like Menzies. A future president of the United States made his career at Gwalia. And Gwalia itself is named for ancient Wales, an ideal homeland that the original investors held to as their heritage. Businesses and careers across the world played on the boom. The price of gold, alongside the costs of processing ore, determined levels of wages and wealth in the goldfields. In the end, the supply or accessibility of gold, all around Menzies, determined the future of the place and its frontier community. Menzies and its people – like the Aboriginals they excluded – lived in a web of connections.

First farms

On the surface of the lake, beyond the oldest of the sisters, and on both sides of that wide bay of the lake, are two incomplete lines of broken fence posts. By the shores, the posts stand up to their full

Abandoned miner's house, Gwalia

height, but as they stretch onto the lake, they disappear: either the mud, sand and salt have drifted high up their sides, or their tops have been worn and battered down. Most of what remains of a fence line are black stumps, fading into the lake: mementoes of another kind of story — of herders and farmers rather than hunters and gatherers or prospectors and miners.

This is a region where no one can own land outside the limits of a town. Miners got exploration leases; those who wished to set up sheep or cattle ranches got pastoral leases. The first sheep and cattle stations in what came to be known as the Eastern Goldfields were set up in the 1870s, in the coastal area about five hundred kilometres south of Menzies. The pastoral frontier did not move far inland before the discovery of gold. Some leases inland were issued in the early 1900s, and between 1910 and 1920 many stations were set up in the land around Menzies. In these years, a tradition of pastoralism took shape that many pastoralists now see as a golden age.

These leases on dry lands, with its mixture of desert and scrub, were large — many of 500,000 acres or more. Three such leases include parts of Lake Ballard: Riverina and Mt Marmion surrounds the west end, Kookynie includes about a third of the north and Jeedamya lies across the east end of the lake. Much of the south shore adjoins a national park and, more recently, an Aboriginal pastoral lease. The land was used for grazing cattle and sheep. Dependent on the vagaries of rain and drought, enough grasses grew to support scattered herds. And the dry, coarse vegetation appeared to many to be ideal for raising sheep for wool.

The family of John and Kath Finlayson held the lease to Jeedamya throughout the heyday of pastoralism, from the 1940s until 1999. The Jeedamya homestead was built in 1920. John's

33

father, A. H. Finlayson, bought it and assumed the lease in 1949. He also bought an abandoned hotel in Malcolm, tore it down and rebuilt the Jeedamya house with the old bricks and timbers. John was born at Jeedamya; Kath married John, and they lived at the station, raising a family, for thirty years. They managed 580,000 acres and ran 12,000 sheep. Some twelve Aboriginals worked for them, which provided support for an Aboriginal community on Jeedamya numbering about fifty.

John and Kath recall their time at Jeedamya as a distinctive and dignified way of life. They relied on special skills, extraordinary resourcefulness. Kath described the annual round of work. April to May was committed to maintenance — especially the upgrading of mills and fixing and extending fences. Jeedamya had 32 water mills, and around double that number of water points. All of this had to be checked and fixed. And there were 390 miles of fences. Shearing was carried out in November and December: all adult sheep would have to be penned, sheared, checked and released — 10,000 in eight weeks meant an average of 180 animals per day. Then all the stock would be moved across the land again, with daily checks on animals, mills and fences in February and March.

We can go to Lake Ballard and see the land, the lake and the society of a sheep station through the eyes of John and Kath Finlayson. Theirs was a particular way of being on the land; they lived and worked there as part of a frontier economy, making changes yet seeking to keep the land productive. Like many others, they looked out on the lake as a place they loved.

As pastoralists and their workers rode out onto the land, mustering or checking fences and windmills, as they found themselves in a leasehold that could be seventy-five miles from one end to another, they must have felt an extreme sense of isolation. So far from the rest of the world, from other parts of Australia, even

Keith Mader, whose million-acre station lies
near the north-west shore of Lake Ballard

from their nearest neighbours. Some of the pride of pastoralists lies in the way this isolation was managed, accepted or overcome. But there were many threads that tied the pastoralists to other, outer worlds. Their fortunes depended on the prices of wool in remote markets; and those markets were at the mercy of events in Europe, Asia and even the Americas: wars, recession, new technologies; changes in the supply and demand for wool and meat across Australia and in international markets. As prices moved on stock exchanges in Tokyo, London and Sidney, pastoralists around Lake Ballard prospered or struggled accordingly. Prices were matched by weather in this set of links; but profit margins and healthy cashflow meant that drought or floods could be coped with. The interplay of economic and international variables led into all the homes on the leasehold lands, and had the power to shape life in them. A history of links between the remotest corner of the most immense station and almost anywhere and everywhere else in the world.

35

Kath Finlayson at the Jeedamya sheep station

First encounters

No one seems sure of the date; it was some time around 1900. The place was Yerilla, east of Menzies. Two prospectors discovered that Aboriginal guides had raided their supplies. Enraged, perhaps by their failure as prospectors as much as by the theft, the two men captured a group of Aboriginal girls, chained them to some trees, and raped them. When the girls' relatives realized what had happened, they attacked the prospectors, hurling spears under cover of darkness. The white men were not hurt, but they counterattacked. They made their way to a nearby water hole, where they killed some thirty people. Word reached the region's police, and the prospectors were arrested and tried for murder. The verdict: justifiable homicide.

This is one of several such stories in the record of early encounters between Aboriginals and miners in the Goldfields region, though the evidence of both the written and oral history record suggests that this kind of murderous confrontation was rare. But the Yerilla episode reveals the extent to which Aboriginals could not look to Australian law to protect them from the excesses of colonists' behaviour. Still less, therefore, could they look to colonial law to protect them from the way colonialism took the land itself into alien ownership and control. Indeed, government attitudes to, and treatment of, Aboriginals from the creation of Western Australia in 1829 until the 1950s can be seen in a series of grim pieces of legislation.

The 1874 Industrial Schools Act gave government the right to detain Aboriginals from infancy up to the age of 21, and the power to confine them to educational institutions. This opened the way for missions and government stations that would take and hold Aboriginal children to 'civilize' them. Then came the Aboriginal Protection Act of 1886 and the Aborigines Act of 1905. One scholar has summarized these as the measures that 'enshrined the contempt and pessimism which in the nineteenth century dominated European attitudes towards Aborigines'. By the 1920s there were about sixty institutions scattered across Western Australia designed to hold, educate and remake Aboriginal children. A common experience for Aboriginals has been the most profound displacement a human being can experience.

The legislation meant to sustain and advance this process continued after the 1920s. The 1936 Native Administration Act

37

introduced yet more laws to increase government control of
Aboriginal life. It also defined children of mixed race as 'Natives'. In
that same year, the Chief Protector of Aborigines, one A. O. Neville,
declared the Kalgoorlie–Boulder townsites 'a prohibited area': all
Aboriginals not in 'legal employment' could be forced out.

A reality of mining is that it does not depend on local labour. So
its frontier does not celebrate, or decry, indigenous peoples. They are
simply absent, or an occasional diversion at the very periphery of
new towns. Not so much a diversion, perhaps, as a form of nuisance:
as the towns sought to change themselves from rough camps and
sprawls of shacks into real, respectable communities, the Aboriginals
who drifted in and out of them received ever more hostile treatment.
According the missionary Schenk, in some of the new towns an
officer had the job, each day at noon, of riding round the streets
driving Aboriginals out of the town boundary, using a whip with
sadistic enthusiasm to achieve best effect.

When it came to the pastoral frontier, the story has been very
different. Large numbers of Aboriginals came to live, and some to
work, on cattle and sheep stations. Both men and women came to be
expert at herding stock, riding and breaking horses, fencing and
maintenance – the core skills needed by the white pastoralists. The
1905 Aborigines Act had anticipated that this would be the most
important source of employment, and had duly insisted that
pastoralists provide their Aboriginal employees with food, clothing
and blankets. No mention was made of wages; and many were paid
little if anything.

The number of Aboriginals working on stations in the Eastern
Goldfields fluctuated between two and three hundred. These may
well be far below the real levels: given the pastoralists' way of hosting
extended families, the difference between a worker and a worker's
relative may have been somewhat blurred. Pastoralists may also have
had an interest in keeping the official numbers low: the law did
require that there be some payment to each worker, albeit in kind
rather than in cash.

Pastoralism became a focus for much Aboriginal life. Those who
wanted to escape the worst kinds of government attention, and who
wished to maintain ritual and ceremonial customs as well as life on
the land, with plenty of 'bush tucker', found many advantages in
living on stations and working with horses, cattle and sheep. Time

could be taken to slip away from the work or from the station itself, and into an Aboriginal territory and Aboriginal world. And pastoralists seem to have seen the advantage to themselves of this balance: a community of workers, living there, available to work long hours doing highly skilled jobs for little or no cash income. Government policy, missionary activity and economic changes from the creation of Western Australia until 1954 resulted in a continuous increase in the number of Aboriginal people who were destitute and despised.

Some of the Aboriginal men and women in Menzies who can speak of the complex and often terrible history of their people are standing, as sculpture, among the Gormley figures on Lake Ballard. We can look at them, and consider what it means to hold such stories, to have this accumulated experience, to be the mouthpiece for a history marred by extremes of racism and abuse. That side of the story can not be forgotten. The other, more recent side of the history, with land claims and hopes of a better deal for Aboriginal people in the region, and in the nation, is also part of their experience. And the Aboriginal people who agreed to be scanned and modelled for the Gormley project did so with immense good humour. Ask them now what they think about the whole process and they roar with laughter and wish only that it be well received and well understood.

When Antony and I met with Paddy, Ron and Ralph at Lake Ballard, Ron asked Antony why he had chosen this particular place. Antony spoke of his wish to have a landscape that was open, large, inspiring. He used the language of aesthetics and art. Ron listened, then asked again, 'But why do you think you came here?' Antony answered with more thoughts about the geography, and the kind of landscape he thought the figures would need. Ron persisted, 'But what led you *here?*'

As I listened to this, I thought that Ron was looking for some reference to destiny, to the spiritual rather than practical or aesthetic explanation. The significance of this project must lie beyond matters of art from the Aboriginal point of view; we were there because we needed to be there, or because history needed us to be there. The need or the history were Aboriginal: the sculptures must take their place in the Aboriginal story — reflecting and addressing that story. Why else would Aboriginal people have agreed to strip naked and

be scanned? Why else would this whole thing be taking place? And, more to the point, why else would Paddy have given permission for this to continue?

In Ron's mind, the project had to lead out of Aboriginal stories. As well as anyone else, Ron acknowledges that Aboriginal and white history, two or more kinds of story, commingle. Ron himself had a white father and was educated at the Mount Margaret Mission. He has worked as a mediator for mining companies in their dealings with Aboriginals who seek to ensure that sacred sites are protected, as well as having taken a leading role in title cases in the Goldfields area. He is a claimant in the Wangkatha case; and a spokesperson in the Wutha claim. His story leads back to Aboriginal life, but also into the lives of miners and pastoralists.

Aboriginals live within a large, frontier community, as well as apart from it. As we look at the figures on the lake, we can not be sure which is and which is not Aboriginal. But half of them are; this is Aboriginal land first and foremost. Land that has been walked for millennia of indigenous life; and land that has been taken and to some extent transformed by colonists. Aboriginal life, throughout living memory, has required, and even depended upon, an entanglement with white Australians. The figures on the lake are entangled, one with another.

Aboriginal Australia evokes a vastness of time and geography; and Aboriginal societies have managed their land and resources in order to keep them, as much as possible, intact, as they have always been. This is the profound conservatism of the hunter-gatherer. Colonial Australia speaks to much shorter spans of time, more specific bits of geography and radical attempts to transform and manage the land. This is the radicalism of farmers. Here lies a dichotomy in human experience: two different and opposed ways of being on this earth.

Edward Johnston, a member of the Wangkatha people

In reality, in the complications and transformations of modern Australian history, Aboriginal people have played their parts inside the frontier – threatened, changed and to some extent shaped by it. The successes and failures of these campaigns have consequences for Aboriginal life everywhere. In recent years, Aboriginal society has also moved in a global arena of indigenous rights and title. Aboriginal peoples around the world have created alliances, political lobbies and the shared project of alerting all nation states to the needs and rights of indigenous peoples.

Linked to the place by the oldest of ties, and informed by stories about the land that reach far back in time and great distances across the region, Aboriginal people in the Menzies area are inseparable from its history. Linked to the outside white world – by the shifting priorities of government policy, changes in economic conditions and human rights campaigns in Europe and North America – Aboriginal life in and around Menzies is also tied to national and global events. The arrival of land claims in Australian politics is a result of debates in Geneva, court cases in Canada and campaigns in the Amazon rainforest. The Wangkatha and Wutha claims in and around Lake Ballard are allied – consciously or unconsciously – to analogous processes in many other parts of the world. We can think about the Aboriginals who now live in Menzies for their links to another kind of culture, a heritage reaching back far, far longer than any colonial story; but we also have to see them within these other communities, a part of a society that came to be called Australia, and defined by its relationship to many other such nations.

41

Aubrey Lynch with his mother Nellie Lynch

From boom to bust and back again

The mining boom had looked as though it would spawn a network of permanent towns; Australia would follow the gold seekers into the western desert. But bust followed boom. By 1930, the mines around Menzies were in the doldrums. People were leaving. The total number of children in the school fell to twenty; two of the classrooms were sold off.

Menzies is now a tranquil little place — except, perhaps, on Friday and Saturday nights when the two bars of the one remaining hotel can burst into modestly drunken, entirely modern noise. Some of the Menzies buildings do evoke a different era. The old hotel, though reduced in all ways from a former grandeur, stands on its original site and is still a place to have your gold weighed and bought. The municipal building, with an elegant façade and fine doorway, stands on the main street. One of its ground-floor rooms is now a library and archive, with many documents from the boom era in rough-and-ready order, a collection of old photographs on the walls and photo albums lying on cabinets of files and documents — an inchoate testimony to another era. The railway line still passes through the edge of the town, and a good if narrow highway leads through the middle of it. There is a scatter of houses around, with a row of small homes built in a short line to one side of the town for Aboriginal families. In 2002, the total population was just 110.

But the gold-mining frontier itself did not die; rather, its character changed. Small, short-term mining replaced the large, vast undertaking. And individual prospecting with a metal detector became a part of life throughout the region. The Eastern Goldfields continued to nurse dreams of bonanzas — smaller ones, perhaps, but nonetheless important. So the movement of men over the land — searching, testing, digging. Within a short walk of the shores of Lake Ballard, prospectors continue to appear and disappear; holes are sunk into the granite and gravel; new seams are found, mined and left. And every weekend, a few men, and sometimes whole families, wander back and forth, much in the style of the hunter-gatherer, following hunches, intuitions and whatever facts can be gleaned ahead of time, waving the sensitized saucer of their metal detectors over swathes of rock and scrub, listening for the vital buzz in the headphones.

43

Opposite: Menzies Hotel
Following pages: Menzies high street

The more serious end of the mining industry in the Menzies area depends on the minimal quantity of gold that can be processed out of ore. For short shafts or small pits, with a mine life of up to six months, five or six grams per ton is the break-even level. The Riverina area mines, just to the south-west of Lake Ballard, have yielded up to 15 grams per ton. But the pockets of rich ore appear to be small; the search for them is difficult, and their lifetime is quite short. To find them, miners have been using a grid of about 200 metres square, and making systematic exploratory test drillings throughout. In 2001–2, this resulted in three new active mining leases near Menzies, two others near Kookynie and one a hundred kilometres farther to the east.

Pastoralists have been less successful. The Finlaysons sold their Jeedamya homestead in 1999. They were bought out by a mining company. So were other stations around Lake Ballard. Miners can survey, test drill and develop ore deposits without having to negotiate with pastoralists' interests. And they can hire a manager, run some stock and think of themselves as spreading their economic lives. In reality, say people like Kath Finlayson, this change of ownership means that the careful pastoralism and agricultural wisdom that once protected the land have gone. Pastoralists from the old school say that now feral goats abound, as do feral cats and dingoes, while awareness of what level of grazing one or another part of a station can bear has more or less disappeared. They also say that Aboriginals who once looked to pastoralists and the stations for work, as home for their families and as a way of balancing ancient customs with employment at the white frontier, have suffered nothing but loss as a result of the equal-rights and fair-pay campaigns fought in their names. Once pastoralists were forced to pay equal wages to their Aboriginal workers, the old system of family support ended, and many Aboriginal families were

Jill Dwyer in the Menzies bar

soon forced off the land and into the grim, destitute and alcoholic fringes of towns. The pastoral community of white leaseholder and cheap labourer families was broken. The mining frontier, they say, is able to seize all.

Memory and nostalgia now lie inside pastoral Australia. The pastoralists among the Gormley figures can stand on Lake Ballard thinking of what this place once meant for them; their gaze can look out at the salt surface of the lake, recalling the occasional, dramatic arrival of banded stilts and the recurrent, routine chase after stray animals in the distance, or towards the shores where their stations once constituted a whole system of life – for themselves, for their little villages of Aboriginal workers and for tens of thousands of domestic animals. In their minds' eyes, as they survey this open landscape – so still, so beautiful to outsiders – they see change and imbalance and loss.

As Antony and I drove towards the western desert, I asked him about how he saw the *Inside Australia* project. He talked not about the genesis of his sculpture, but about the origins of sculpture itself. He spoke of 'the first gesture of sculpture' in which a stone upright activates a place, giving meaning and consciousness, making a human something out of a natural nothingness. In this way, he said, sculpture 'animates'; yet it is also static, and we have to accept its two qualities: inertia – a body that never moves, and often lies down on the earth – and silence – the sculpture, though giving meaning to place, is mute.

'Stillness and silence. And what we have to do is make stillness and silence count', he said. 'Make a body that in a way is like death; willingly go to the place of death and inertia, and then be released into the other side. That's what I'm interested in.'

47

Above: View of Menzies showing the hotel
Following pages: Views of Menzies

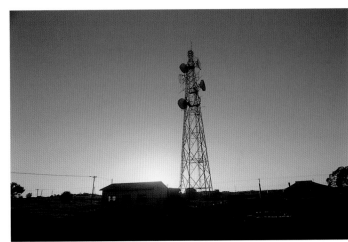

So he finds Lake Ballard, from the air. A place of immense beauty and yet indifferent? With the stillness and silence of nature? He was aware that Aboriginal peoples will have known this place as their land, as a social and cultural space. But from the air, and perhaps also from the land, when visiting for the first time, there are few signs of human presence. A timelessness, rather. Antony had read that in this part of Australia there is faultline of limestone rock, with outcrops that are approximately 1.5 billion years old. Is it this silence that causes him to want to set up his figures, to leave his handprint on an apparent eternity, to make meaning in defiance of a sense of meaninglessness that vast spans of time cause us to feel?

I think not. From the beginning, Antony envisaged a community of figures. He may not have known what the community was going to be, quite who they were. But he was committed, from the start, to representing, in some way, their meanings, or the meanings their minds and lives give to Lake Ballard. They would stand vertical, and seem to stretch to a far, white horizon. The appeal of the salt lake came from this space and whiteness: figures could stand here with immense effect. Also, this wide, white world might be able to evoke something about the human condition: the eternity in which we stand, as minute structures, with strength enough just to stand. The condition of ultimate nakedness could be imagined here; and the extreme of the landscape could, as metaphor, as image, strip away not just our clothes, but also our gesture, our appearance. Antony's vision was a community of people at Lake Ballard whose internal selves, an inner core of human structure, would be visible.

Yet he did not imagine them as trapped in any ultimate silence — no more so, this is to say, than is inherent to sculpture. Against the scale of Lake Ballard, even at full human height, they would be small; reduced to their cores, they would be black, steel, vertical, but appear as slender threads in the brilliant light. Yet they would have their stories. From the point of view of Australian history and Eastern Goldfields society, this is a sculpture project on a contested, not an empty space. The Gormley figures come from each side of the contest, representing a community whose combined experience and eruptive bitterness speak to much that is deep inside Australia.

This is also a project that raises questions about what Antony Gormley imagines, intends and fears for the work. The second night we camped at Lake Ballard, I asked Antony some of these questions about the *Inside Australia* project. I put it to him that this was work that depended on people knowing rather a lot. He said, 'Maybe the first thing that has to be said is that reasonable art comes from a degree of reason, therefore you don't get good art without some form of good thinking.'

We break through the salt surface of the lake, get into the viscous mud, among the dormant brine shrimps, only when we begin to listen to the stories. So we may need to know at least some part of this, have some sense of what the figures are whispering, as we see and walk among them. So I asked Antony how he put together his sense that art is what the person looking does and an installation that has led him so far into a web of societies in and around Menzies. What does he want people to know in order to see this particular piece of work? He replied, 'I would like to say: all they need to know is to leave everything behind. A lot of what I have been trying to do in the work is about trying to leave myself behind. You might say that this is a rather elaborate distancing from the context – distancing, I mean, from the usual contexts in which you might find art: at home, in the museum, at the gallery, in the private collection, whatever. But the disengagement from natural habitat in the ecosystems of the art world is an attempt to avoid pre-meditation. So when you ask that question, I answer: the best thing that people can have with them is their eyes and their bodies and, I hope, a relatively open mind. And I think with this bit of the real world, which has temporarily, or for a longer time, taken possession of my work, will effect them. And I think if they just really look, I would like to feel that they need to know nothing.'

I was not sure that this was the complete answer. Antony himself had become more and more engaged with the people of Menzies, their histories, their societies. He may have begun the work by looking down from the window of a small plane onto a white and empty salt lake, a kind of blank canvas, whose glare and long horizons and apparent remoteness and emptiness suggested a perfect location for a spread of figures. His imagination may have been excited by images of steel, reduced sculptures on hard, white salt lake, and figures that would spread towards a seemingly infinite distance. But the project had led from a sense of a blank and perfect canvas to meeting men, women and children whose place in different kinds of history gives them particular kinds of relationships to the place.

To go 'inside Australia', under the crust of the salt lake, is to get to know more and more about these people; and therefore to have an ever more detailed and enriched sense of who they are, where they come from; and thereby to begin to have ideas of what they represent. *Inside Australia* is not a set of pure images; at least, if it exists to be looked at, it also can best be looked at through eyes with a mind that is informed by many kinds of knowledge. There was a moment when Antony and I were standing together at the top of Snake Hill, at the peak of the oldest of the seven sisters on the lake, looking out at the perfect site for his sculptures, when he said, 'I want to create a new kind of art, an anthropological art.'

I don't think that there has been anything 'too easy' about the *Inside Australia* project. Not easy to make, not easy to know, and not easy to visit. To make the journey to Lake Ballard, to walk on the salt lake among the figures, to travel great distances — on the surface of the world, in history, and with the imagination — this is the commitment that Antony Gormley invites, but does not expect. He has made an intense and extensive exploration, of a medium and of a place. Perhaps you can leave everything behind, and arrive with the baggage shed, the mind open and the spread of figures there in front of you, amazing in an amazing landscape. And perhaps, in this state of mind, aware of being at an edge, under a burning sun, seeing the shapes, the colour, the lack of colour, the mind can dive inside Australia, finding an intuitive trail beneath the surface, trusting to the power of work and place to act on the strange, ineffable human mind. This is a way of coming to the Lake Ballard project.

But if you will, you can also come here as historian and anthropologist. You can travel to each of the communities, follow the trails left by different kinds of history, and see inside the sculptures, and imagine their minds — stirring your own mind with thoughts about Australia, and yet having room, nonetheless, for the mind's

Antony Gormley on his first visit to Lake Ballard

imaginative freedom. In this way the journey is a meeting of minds: yours with the work, and with the maker of the work, and with all that we can know about the people who stand, in effigy, on the lake. The figures on Lake Ballard are from one community – the people who live in or near Menzies. You can look at the figures and imagine them reaching back in time, to first steps taken on the lake; and with voices that could be heard and understood, relaying their stories, far across Australia. They stand still and isolated in a remote and silent place; they have links, in the mind's eye, with peoples and places hundreds of miles and thousands of years away. But between them – Aboriginal and European together – they stand on many kinds of land, in all kinds of history, with various and rival stories. As you look at them and imagine their voices, perhaps you will hear both conflict and reconciliation. Either way, trusting to an innocence of view or looking to some forms of history and anthropology, when you come to Lake Ballard and spend time with the Gormley sculptures, you will be able to think about what it means to stand inside Australia.

53

View of Lake Ballard from Snake Hill before the installation of *Inside Australia*

The Making of Inside Australia

MENZIES HOTEL
— EST 1902 —

MINIMUM DRESS

Shirt,shorts
& Thongs

Thank you

Scanning the People

Shelagh Magadza

Scanning the residents of Menzies took place over a busy four days in June 2002. The scanner had arrived from California via Perth and we had only a short time to use it before it went on to its final destination at Fox Studios in Sydney. It was also our first chance to engage the media in the project and allay the scepticism it had provoked in Perth. A major installation in the 'middle of nowhere' had not yet captured the imagination of many Western Australians. Our arrival in Menzies, with an entourage of technicians, reporters, photographers and film crew, was hardly low key. Not a reassuring sight for people who were being asked to take their clothes off.

While the scanner was being assembled in the town hall, we set about knocking on doors to ask people to participate in the project. Antony had been to Menzies once before and had talked to the locals about what he hoped to do. However, they still had only a limited understanding of what the process and end result would be. The first step, taking your clothes off and having your naked image scanned, was the source of much hilarity, followed by a non-committal attitude. Antony explained and explained and drew pictures, but in the end we kept coming back to the nakedness.

Once the scanner was installed, we held a demonstration and invited the townsfolk to come and see how it would work. Only a few came. Antony went through the process himself, having his body scanned to demonstrate the privacy they would enjoy. Again, there was much hilarity and later, in the pub, people rolled their eyes and described Antony as 'arty farty', insinuating that it would take a lot more to get normal people like themselves to take their clothes off. The pub, established in the boom year of 1902, has a minimum dress code of shirt, shorts and thongs.

The evening before we were due to scan the people of Menzies, we still had no assurance from anyone that they would participate. Antony was by then visibly worried and, according to one local, behaving like 'a galah on a fencepost'. Despite having a contingency

The sign on the front window of Menzies hotel and pub

plan in Perth, where we were to scan another sixty people at the University of Western Australia (just in case), it was important to all of us to have the participation of the local community. It was a fundamental part of what we were trying to do.

The next day sixty-nine people presented themselves for scanning. The first were two English backpackers we'd met playing cards in the pub. Then came the policeman and the school teacher. After that, the whole Menzies Mob swung into action, galvanized by the efforts of two people: Kath Finlayson, President of the Shire Council, and Ian Tucker, Manager of the Menzies Aboriginal Centre. Kath and Ian had gone from family to family talking up Menzies' civic pride and encouraging (I suspect in some cases telling) people to be scanned.

The mini-census that we conducted over that winter Saturday was a wonderful snapshot of the community. Patterns of age and relationships emerged as the constant stream of people and prams arrived at the town hall: the three-year-old who flapped her arms and created an angelic and unusable scan; the Scotsman who had fallen off a wagon and stayed in Menzies; and the station owner who had driven eighty kilometres from the 500,000-square-kilometre station where he lived alone. Although, on the face of it, all that each of them had given us was an image, it was the accompanying stories that made the gesture so much more meaningful.

Above: Bob and Christine Earnshaw, Emily and friends arrive at the town hall to be scanned

Waiting to be scanned. A total of 131 people were scanned in Menzies and later in Perth.

Antony explaining the scanning process

The scanning required each person to undress and stand in the scanning cubicle for the seventeen seconds needed for the four lasers/cameras to pass from top to bottom and capture the three-dimensional geometry of the body form.

Bob Earnshaw awaits his turn. No male was to be present in the room while the women were scanned, and vice versa.

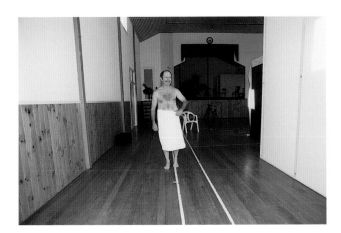

Bob after being scanned. At the end of the process, each person had their own full-body scan with half a million digital coordinates (see pages 61–5).

The scanning process was devised and operated by technicians from headus (metamorphosis) in Perth. Kevin, a small mute boy, was entranced by the technology and soon became proficient at running the scanner.

Lorraine Williams describes the experience of being scanned and then seeing a digital rendering
of herself and her friends (opposite and following pages).

Back at headus in Perth, the scans went through a post-processing process that the technicians
dubbed 'gormleyization'. Horizontal cross-sections were taken through each body
and the form reduced by two thirds at those points.

When all the points were connected and the contours joined, the result was an Insider.
Despite this transformation, each individual could still be identified from their 'gormleyized' figure.
Its shape was the same height but had one third of their body volume. One of the 'gormleyized' scans
appears on pages 64–5. Once they had been through this process, the digital files
were then sent to a polystyrene mill in Sydney to be turned into computer-routed patterns that
would be assembled into figures at the foundry in Perth ready for casting.

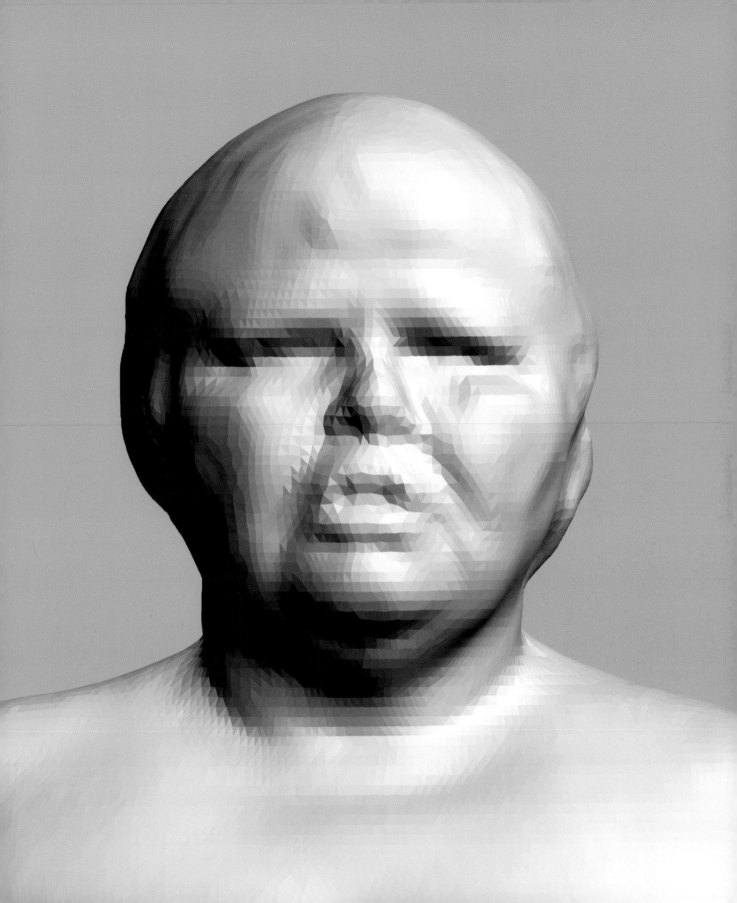

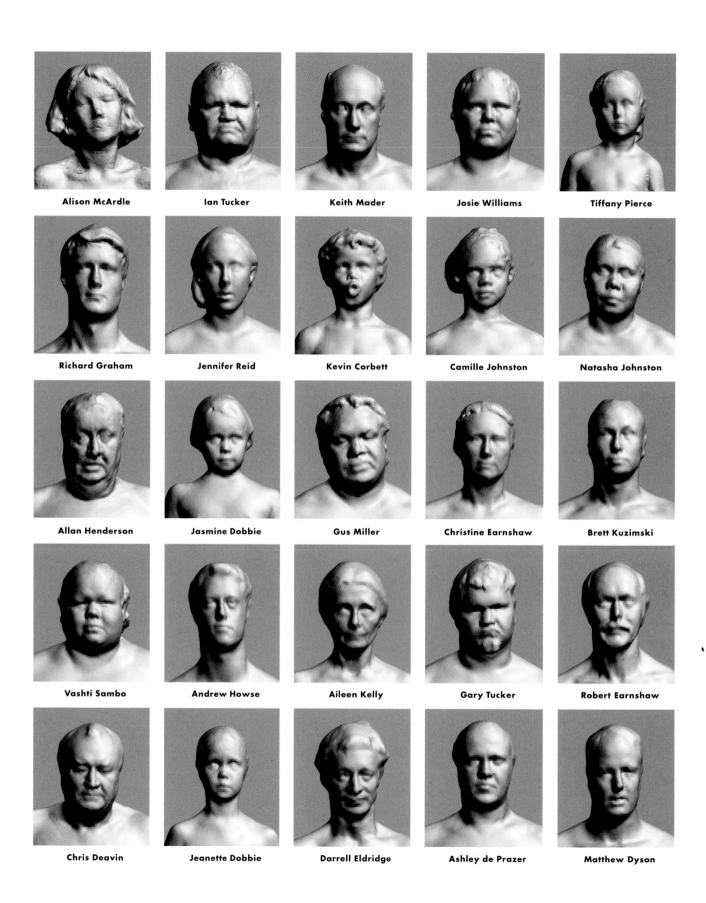

Alison McArdle   Ian Tucker   Keith Mader   Josie Williams   Tiffany Pierce

Richard Graham   Jennifer Reid   Kevin Corbett   Camille Johnston   Natasha Johnston

Allan Henderson   Jasmine Dobbie   Gus Miller   Christine Earnshaw   Brett Kuzimski

Vashti Sambo   Andrew Howse   Aileen Kelly   Gary Tucker   Robert Earnshaw

Chris Deavin   Jeanette Dobbie   Darrell Eldridge   Ashley de Prazer   Matthew Dyson

Phillip Parker

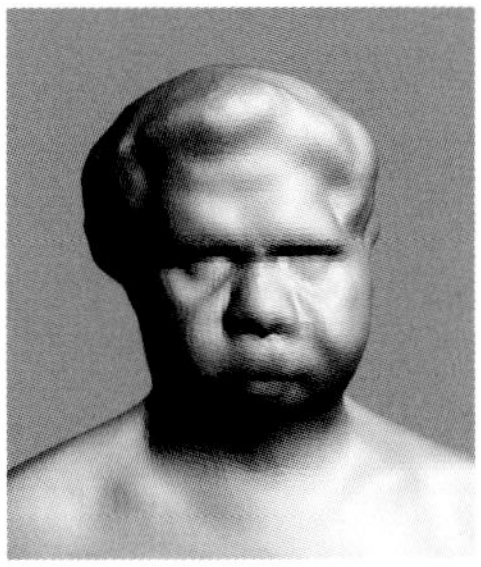

Simon Jones

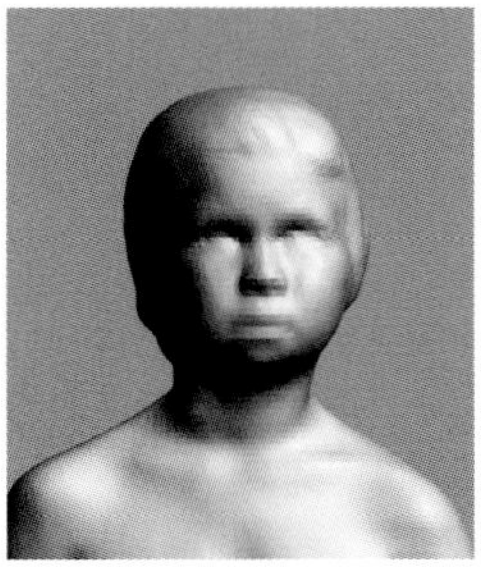

Kellie Tucker

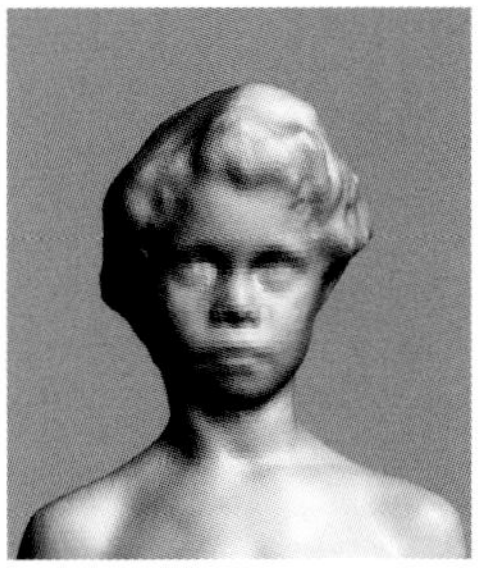

Nathan Corbett

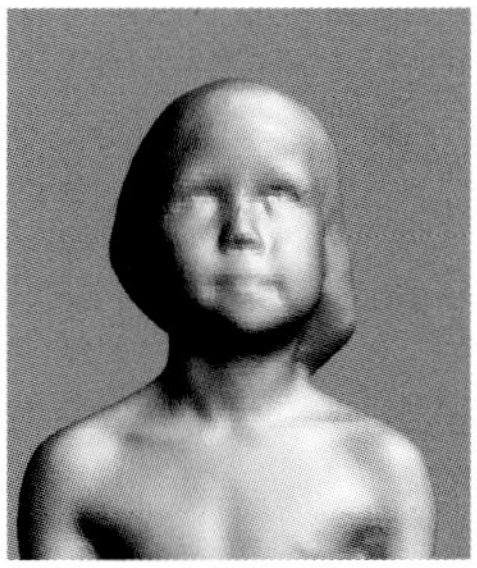

Kyra Shepherd

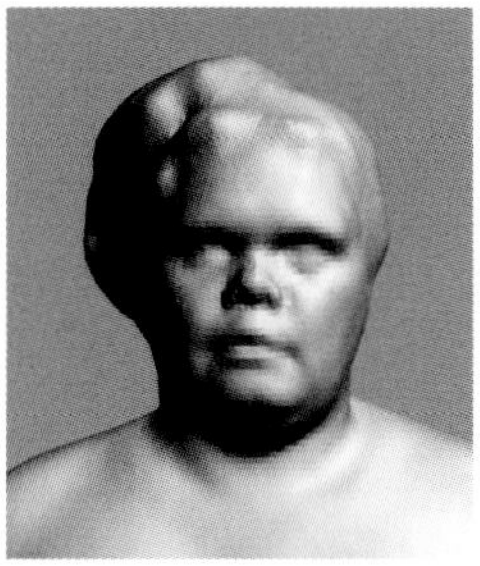

Louise Johnston

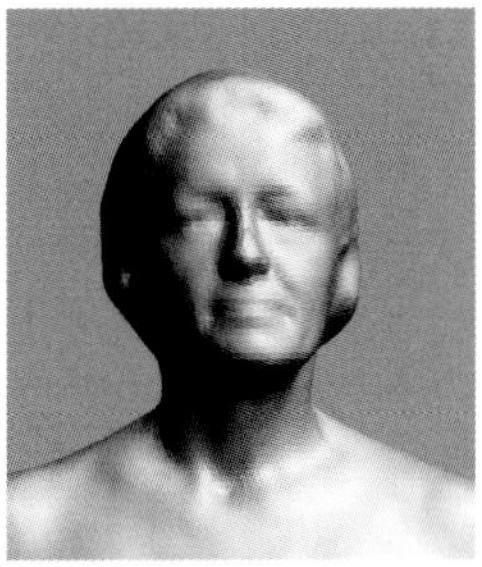

Jill Dwyer

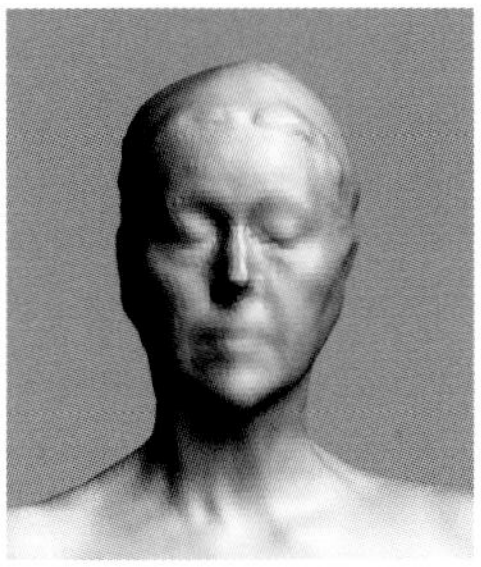

Samantha Mazza

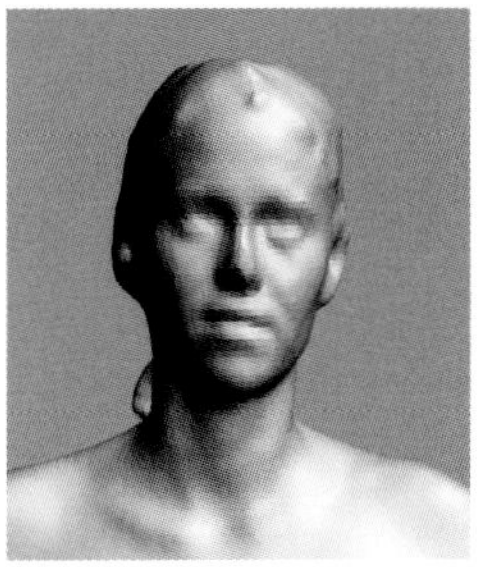

Rachel McAuliffe

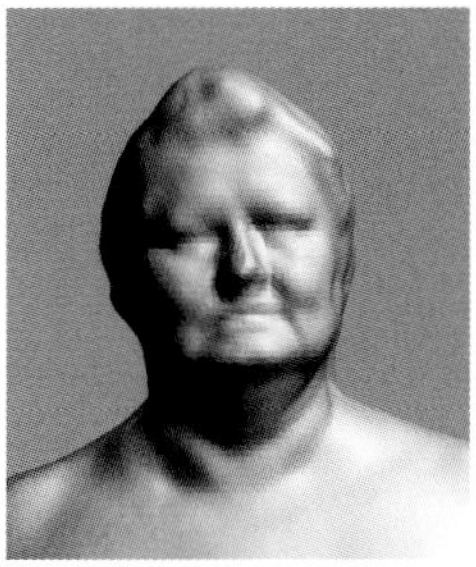

Janet Henderson

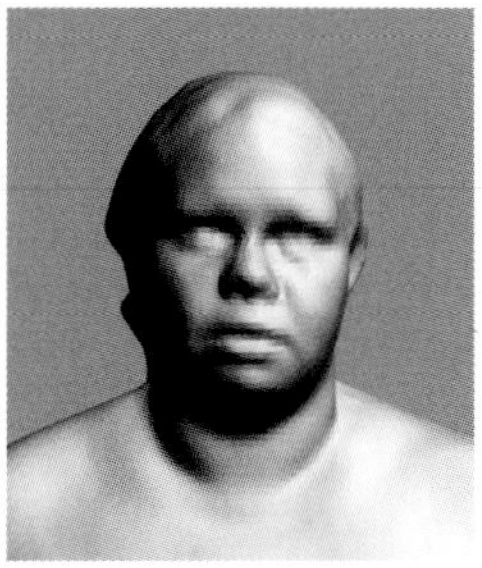

Deanne Blizzard

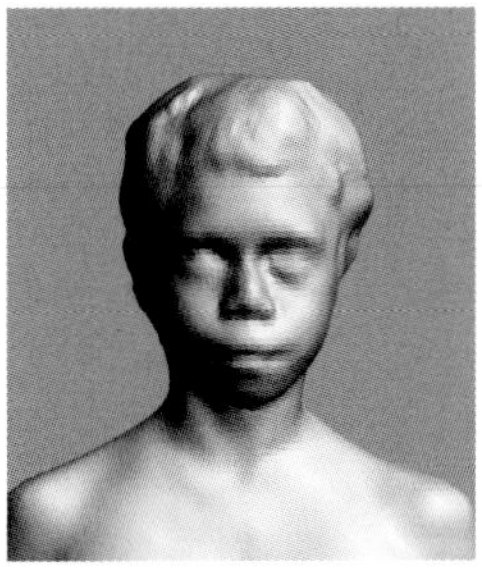

Jayden Johnston

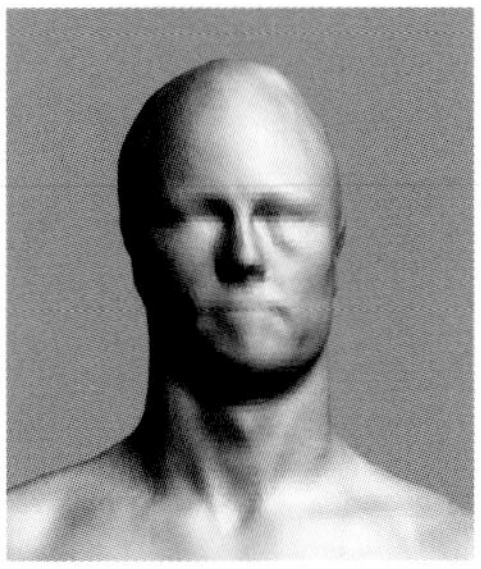

Rob Money

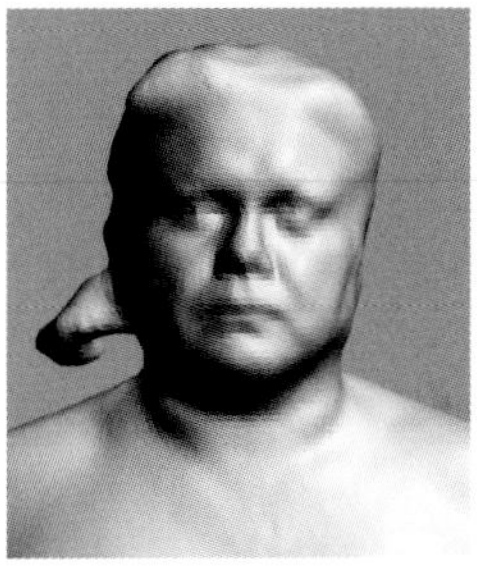

Ross Cashin

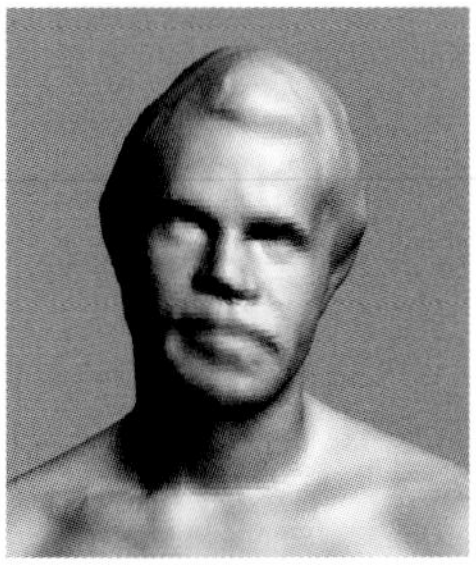

Chadwick Tucker

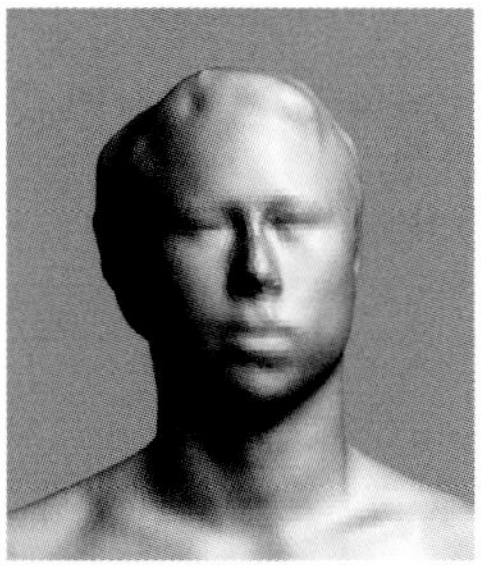

John Reid

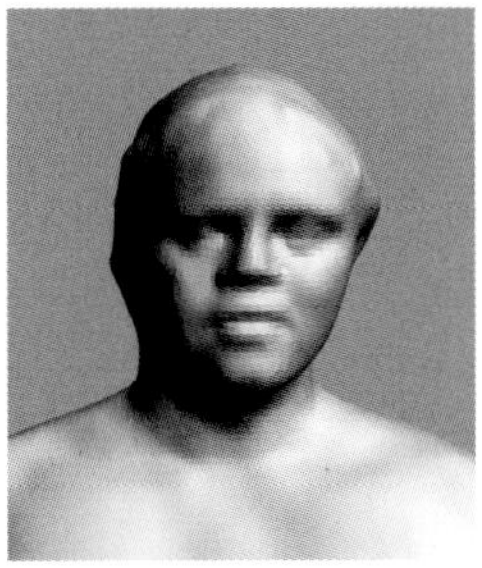

Alana Cameron

John Finlayson

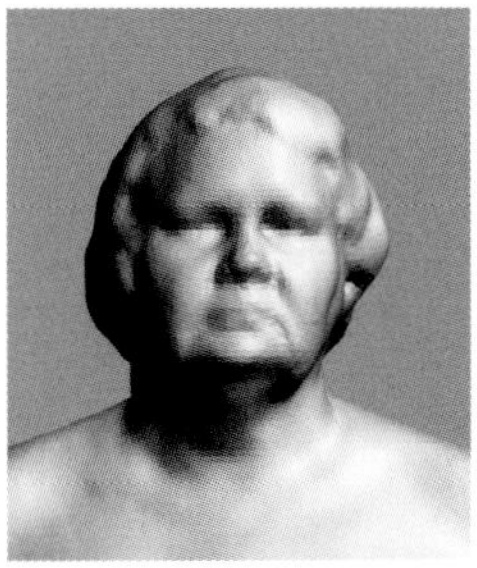

Joan Tucker

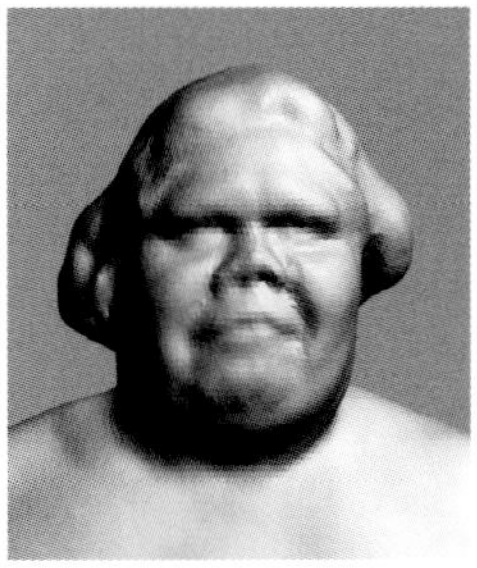

Anthea Johnston

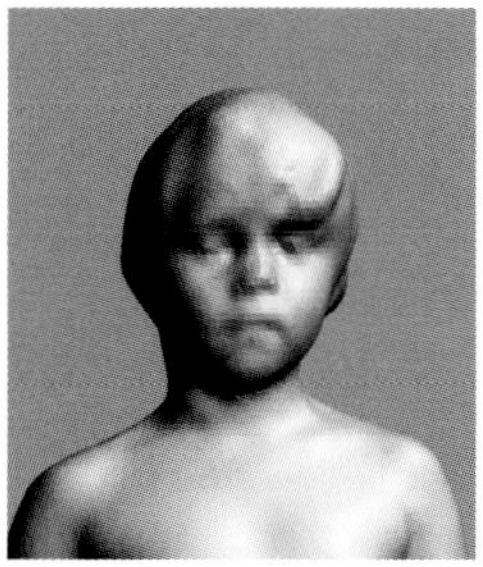

Danielle Brennan

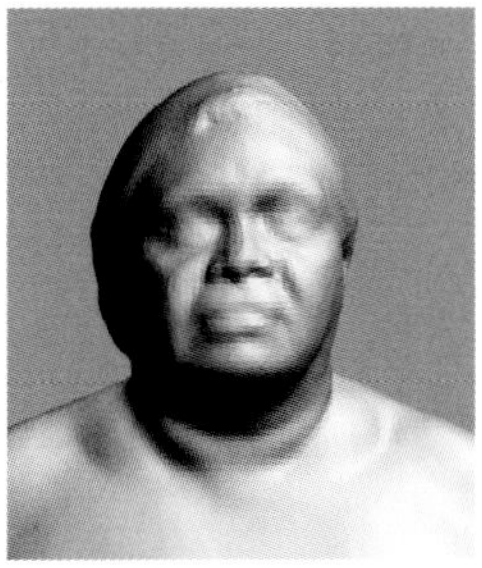

Estelle Blizzard

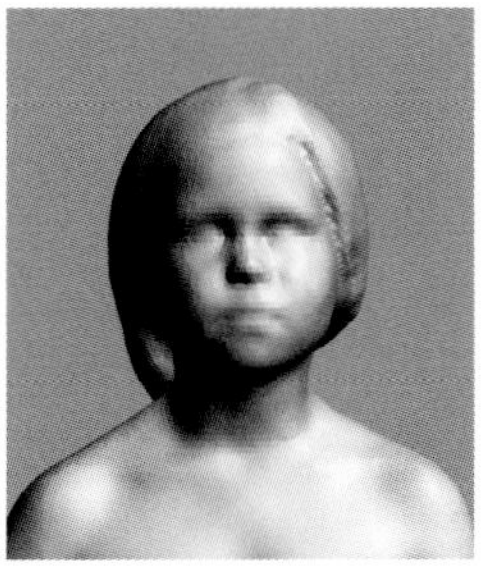

Kaylene Tucker

Kath Finlayson

Tracey Milner

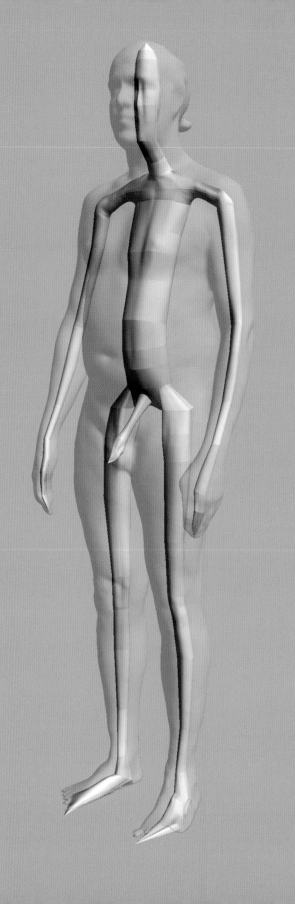

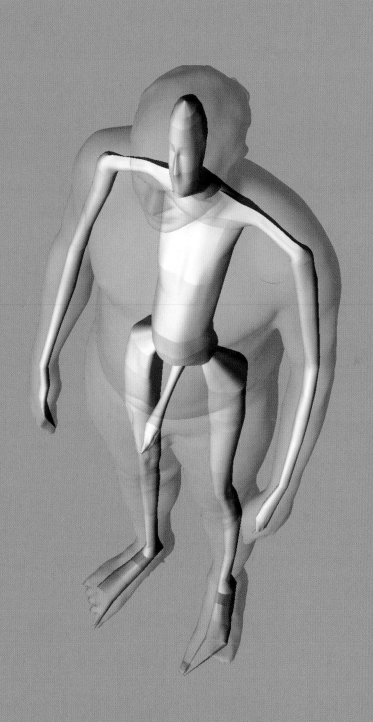

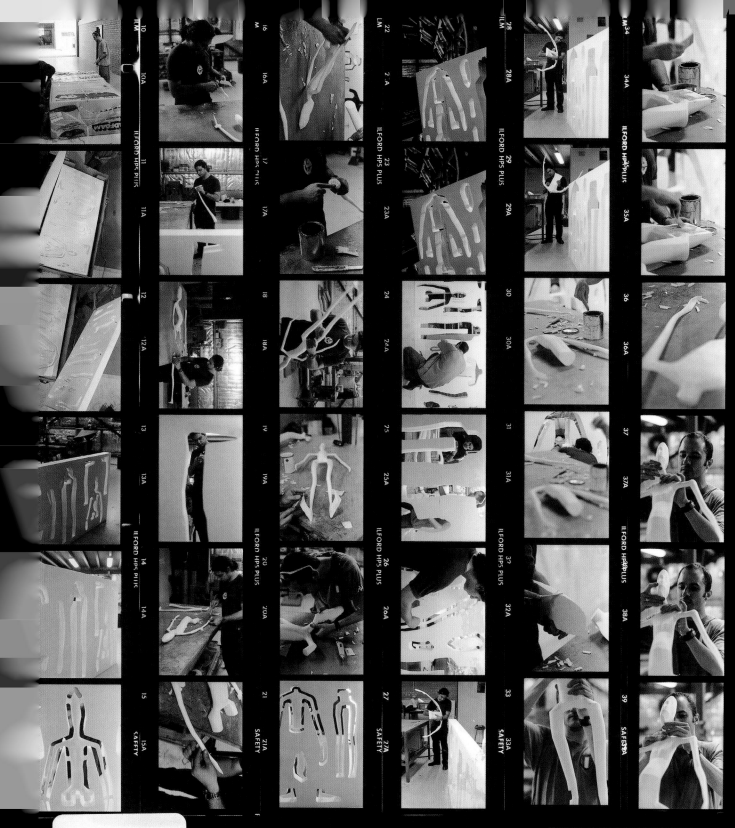

INSIDE AUSTRALIA
Lake Ballard / Antony Gormley

C-498-24

Making the Insiders

Finn Pedersen

During the fabrication of the Insiders, I was to be Antony's eyes in the VEEM foundry in Perth. I was to inspect, document and instruct the fabrication crew, and send digital photos of the whole process back to Antony so he could ensure quality. The factory was a strange combination of the twenty-first century and the Iron Age. Modern induction furnaces melted ingots of pure metals; the alloys formed were checked with a mass spectrometer, which measures the masses and relative concentrations of atoms and molecules; and temperatures were maintained with a two-decimal-point accuracy. But at the moment of the pour you were transported back in time – to the primordial wonder of flame and molten metal, of exploding gases and fountains of sparks. The foundry workers were powerful Wagnerian figures with leather aprons, beards to their chests and polycarbonate headware. They were steady among the fire and glowing liquids.

The process of making the sculptures was relatively simple. The computer-routed polystyrene patterns arrived from Sydney, packed like a giant model aeroplane kit. The parts of each figure were cut out and assembled, and polystyrene runners fixed between the limbs and body to allow the metal to flow through the whole piece. 'In-gate' risers through which to pour the liquid were attached to the shoulders and backs of the figures, and vents to allow gases to escape; footplates were added to attach the footings that would support the figures on the salt lake. Over several days the patterns were put together in this way. Digital images of each figure were referred to constantly, to ensure the accuracy of the patterns.

Once assembled, the approved figures were taken down to the foundry floor for moulding. They were to be moulded face up and cast face down. A 2.4m x 1.2m x 0.6m plywood box was set up on the concrete floor of the moulding area. The in-gate risers were laid down first, and then the figure was placed on top of those.

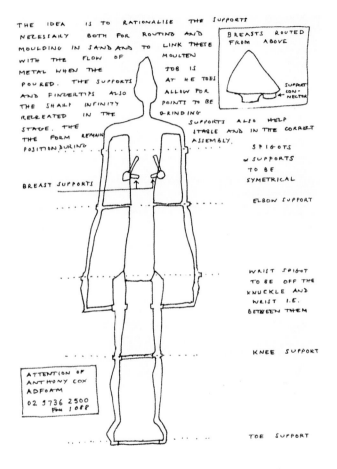

THE IDEA IS TO RATIONALISE THE SUPPORTS
NECESSARY BOTH FOR ROUTING AND
MOULDING IN SAND AND TO LINK THESE
WITH THE FLOW OF MOULTEN
METAL WHEN THE JOB IS
POURED. THE SUPPORTS AT HE TOES
AND FINGERTIPS ALSO ALLOW FOR
THE SHARP INFINITY POINTS TO BE
RETREATED IN THE GRINDING
STAGE. THE SUPPORTS ALSO HELP
THE FORM REMAIN STABLE AND IN THE CORRECT
POSITION DURING ASSEMBLY.

BREASTS ROUTED FROM ABOVE

SUPPORT CONNECTOR

SPIGOTS
& SUPPORTS
TO BE
SYMETRICAL

BREAST SUPPORTS

ELBOW SUPPORT

WRIST SPIGOT
TO BE OFF THE
KNUCKLE AND
WRIST I.E.
BETWEEN THEM

KNEE SUPPORT

ATTENTION OF
ANTHONY COX
ADFOAM
02 9736 2500
FAX 1088

TOE SUPPORT

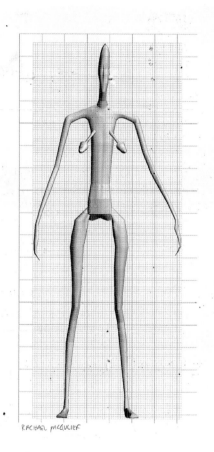

RACHAEL McAULIEF

Above left: Antony's instructions to the polystyrene manufacturers.
Above right: First digital rendering of Rachel McAuliffe.
Opposite: Polystyrene Insiders awaiting sand moulding.

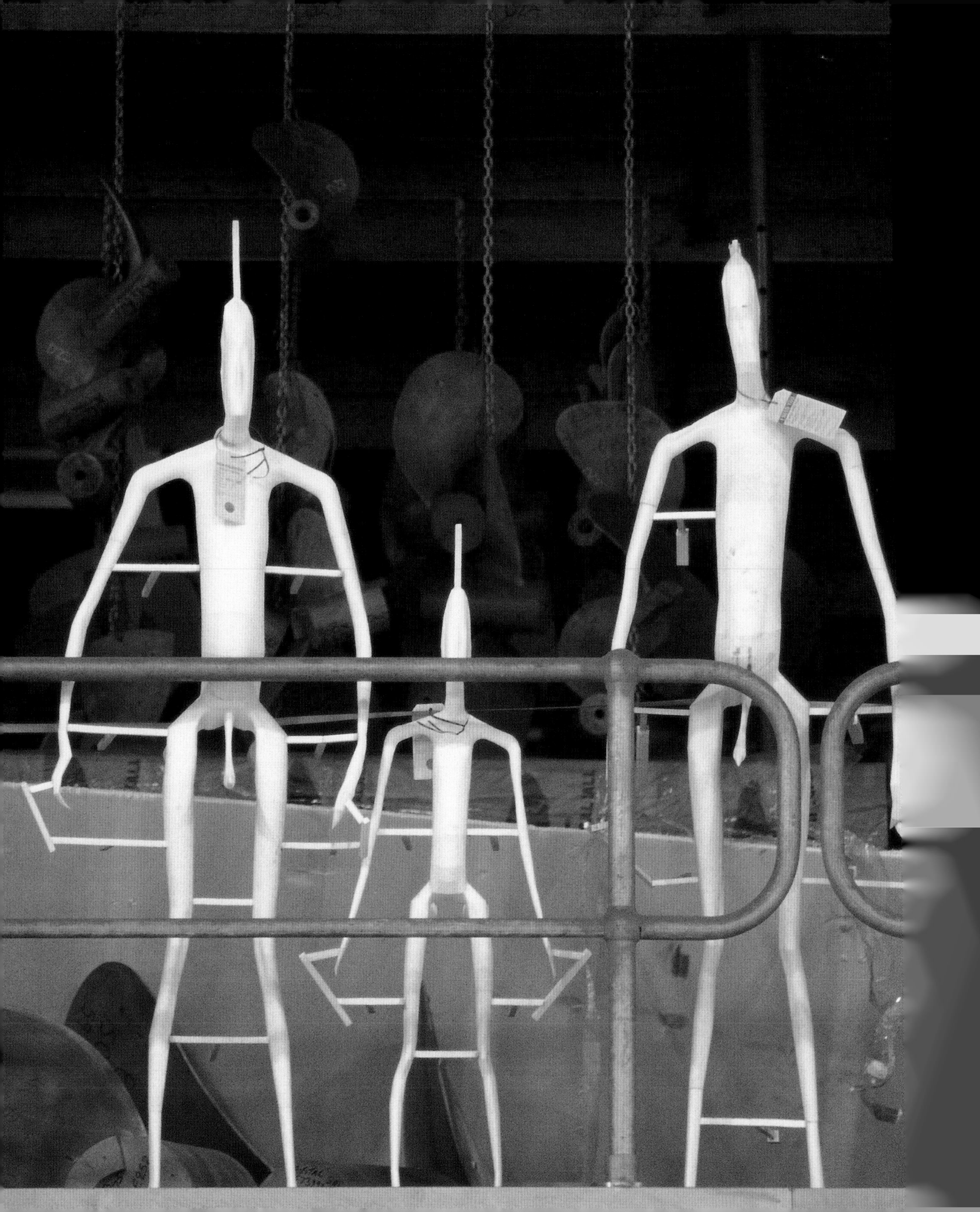

Measurements were then taken of the centre of the forehead, the tips of the hands and feet, the chest, breasts and penises to monitor and control any distortion during the moulding. Silica and zircon casting sand, damp with phenolic-setting resin, were then poured around the figure, carefully built up in layers, and compressed by hand. A finer refractory sand was placed against the polystyrene to ensure a smoother cast surface. The finished mould was then allowed to harden for at least a day before being cast. The sand turned pink as it set and transformed into a kind of sandstone.

The casting was carefully choreographed and spectacular. The moulds were lined up like many strange sarcophagi. A reservoir of casting sand and metal shields was assembled, cylinders of refractory material inserted in openings to keep the metal hot, and a ceramic filter placed over the in-gate to catch any slag or impurities from the ladle. The melt itself took hours to prepare. Ingots of stainless steel were placed in the induction furnaces and the temperature was constantly monitored. Once the correct temperature was reached (1555 °C), a team of casters assembled: one on the furnace tilt control, one on the wheel of the ladle, one on the gantry crane controls, one with a digital thermometer like a high-tech witch's broom. The ladle had been placed in front of a gas jet to preheat it.

Carefully, the furnace crucible was tipped over the ladle and a little metal poured in to ensure it was as hot as the metal inside the crucible. This metal was returned to the furnace, heated a little further and finally poured back into the ladle, to be rapidly swung over a mould for the pour. One last temperature check, then the wheel was spun, the metal poured into the reservoir, vaporizing the polystyrene into helium and carbon dioxide, sometimes exploding to send a shower of sparks over the crew. Hot metal ran over the mould; vents spewed forth flame and gas; the crew poured sand over the hot rivulets to solidify them. When I was finally allowed on the floor, dressed in

Opposite: Sand moulding an Insider at the VEEM Foundry, Perth
Above: Pouring in the molten stainless-steel alloy

safety gear, to document the melt, I was told not to move if the metal ran over my feet – it would be worse wherever I jumped.

The moulding had been like a strange archaeological dig in reverse; the casting, some scene from Valhalla; the breaking-out, a brutal birthing with sledgehammers and jackhammers. After a day or so cooling, the cast moulds were lifted to one corner of the foundry floor, where they were unceremoniously broken out from the pink sandstone with brute force. Slowly the figures emerged with their runners and risers attached, like folded mechanical angel wings. All these extraneous metal pieces, as well as the runners between the torso and limbs, were cut off with a grinding disk – a process called 'fettling'. The fettler was instructed to leave a 1–1.5mm-high 'scar' in place – a mark of fabrication. In some cases, shrinkage had caused in-gate pockets and had cracked some limbs. Several limbs of the child figures were severed and had to be welded back together, with reference to the original digital images. These faults were retained as marks of production.

The fettled figures were then trucked to a heat-treatment plant, where they were loaded into stainless-steel trays and fork-lifted into large, double-sided furnaces and heated to 1050 °C, removed after thirty minutes and air-cooled under fans. The sight of the grey figures being loaded into the furnace and then removed bright orange was moving and eerie. Observing the figures being created, destroyed, transformed and transmuted was an almost spiritual experience, sometimes delightful and sometimes almost horrific.

The last part of the fabrication was the fitting of the footings. Then the figures were loaded onto a flatbed road-train for their journey to Lake Ballard. In my mind's eye, I saw them hurtling down Great Eastern Highway, following the serpentine silver pipe that transports water from Mundaring Weir to Kalgoorlie, then to Menzies whence they came.

Previous pages: Just after pouring Bob Earnshaw's Insider.
Above: Breaking out the sculpture.
Opposite: Fettling. Following pages: Heat-treating the Insiders.

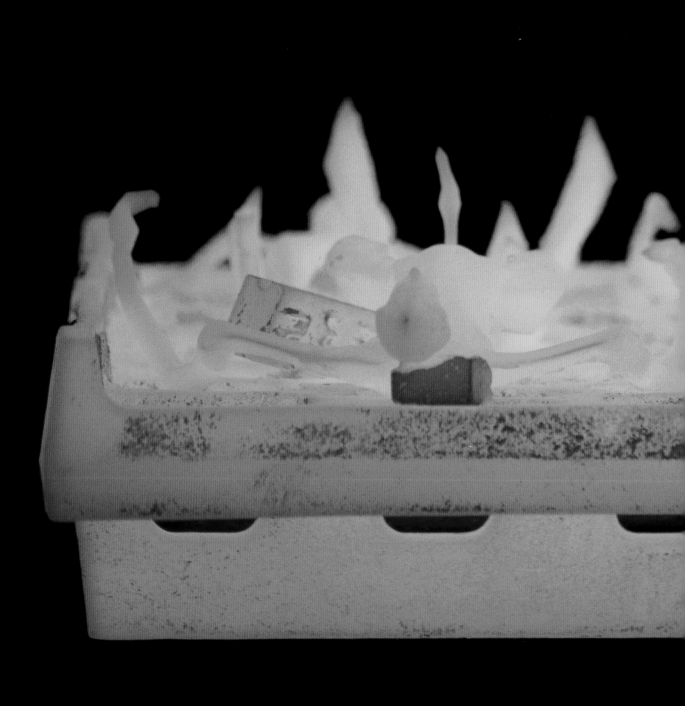

The Installation

Finn Pedersen

The approach to Lake Ballard from Menzies passes through a classic Eastern Goldfields landscape of small salt lakes, swamps and mixed woodlands of mulga, western myall, eucalypt and grevilleas. When the installation team arrived in early December, the grevilleas were flowering, with long cream flower-heads, and when we left some nine days later the mulga were dressed in bright yellow flowers.

A long, low range called Snake Hill runs north to south at the western edge of the lake, lying like a body on the flat woodlands. Five hundred metres to the north, off the Menzies–Sandstone road, four kilometres back from the Snake Hill Road intersection, is the site. Just offshore rises the dome-shaped mound — perhaps an ancient, eroded magma plug. The laterite plain leads from the road to the low gypsum sandhills at the edge of the lake, then to the clay lake-edge colonized by red-purple and emerald-green samphire communities. Some fifty metres, out the samphire gives way to the seemingly barren salt pan.

After rain the lake can be a mirror of the sky, or a pink leather surface, carrying the marks of cattle, kangaroos, birds and reptiles. After the sun has burnt the water away, a salt rime forms. It starts out in the deeper waters of the lake and seems to make its way towards the shore. The salt is like a living thing. Its crystals constantly form, dissolve and reform. When I was a few kilometres offshore during the middle of one of our hottest days, the crystals made noises that I had only heard in the mangroves of the Kimberley at low tide — popping, sucking and clicking sounds. At different times, the crystals looked like octagonal coins floating over fine snow; or giant sperm pointing their tails to the prevailing winds; or fine, hairlike tubes; or long, raised fault-lines; or rain-weathered snow. Strange iridescent-green beetles with long golden legs run at high speed over the crystalline surface. Spiders make their homes in holes. Cockroaches become caught in the salt crystals and petrified.

After the casting, my next role was to help select and supervise a team of volunteers who would work with four staff members from the Perth International Arts Festival, Thunderbox (a documentary film crew directed by Hugh Brody), and Antony. Our eighteen volunteers came from France, Indonesia, Malaysia, Australia and New Zealand. They included high-school students and under-graduates studying architecture, poetry, English literature and art. They worked together and with the artist as a motivated and thoughtful team. The town of Menzies accommodated all of us in a semi-ruined hotel, the house of a local prospector (one of the Insiders), and the local pub.

On our first day on site we set up a base camp in a depression in the sand dunes, sheltered by a grove of mulga trees and guarded by a metre-long barney, a burrow-dwelling lizard who became the camp cleaner. The camp was to become the breakfast kitchen, nursing post and control centre of the operation, and, with Adam and Rupert, the camp cooks, the foundation of the team's morale.

The road-train arrived, and two nine-kilolitre polypropylene water tanks were unloaded to provide water for future visitors. The Insiders were tethered to an open flatbed trailer, covered in scraps of carpet and dusted with red dirt from the journey. The figures were removed from the truck, laid side by side and covered with carpet to shade them from the summer sun.

The surface of the figures was a deep charcoal colour, and sandpaper rough to touch. We wore leather gloves to protect our hands from blisters and cuts, and from the heat that the figures soaked up. The lightest figure weighed about 16 kilograms; the heaviest, 131 kilos; most were around 50 or 60 kilograms. Moving the figures was backbreaking work. Teams of up to five people lifted the heavier figures from the road-train, lowered them to the ground and then lifted them onto a ute. They were then driven five hundred metres to the fore-dune at the edge of the lake. There they were laid out, with their U-shaped steel footings alongside, and Antony carefully inspected each one, making notes as to size and gender. One of the figures was selected and two PIAF staff members, Drew Dymond and Todd Westbrook, demonstrated how to install the footings, level and bolt on the figures, and then how to treat the bolts to make them more difficult to remove.

Breakfast at the installation camp

88

Unloading the Insiders on the edge of Lake Ballard and
covering them wth carpet to protect them from the sun

89

Antony checks the Insiders and gives the team of volunteers a final
pep talk as they prepare for the installation

On the second day, Antony and I walked out onto the lake and placed survey flags on the surface, indicating the positions for the first figures. Antony knew exactly where he wanted to place them, but at about three kilometres out the lake became too boggy to proceed, so the plan was modified. He counted steps, spacing the figures between three and six hundred paces apart. He avoided forming a line of figures. No figure could face another figure. A fan-shaped field was formed, some two and half kilometres deep and three and half kilometres wide.

The positions were reported to shore by radio, and six teams set off into the lake with the first figures. Each team consisted of four or five volunteers with an orange 'brickies' trolley', a sledgehammer, spanners, a trowel, water, a two-way radio and sun protection. The brickies' trolley is a small steel cart with two wide pneumatic wheels, normally used to carry a load of bricks. The wheels of the trolley marked the lake surface slightly, except when the mud was very wet and the trolleys became sleds. From our vantage point on the top of the mound, we could see the lines of the trolleys snaking out across the plain, like crabs on a beach, ending at a faint figure.

The daily routine required us to get to site at dawn. Antony and I would walk on the lake for about two or three hours, placing markers, usually six at a time. Each team would move out onto the lake and install a figure, have breakfast at about 7.30am, install another figure and leave the site by 11am, when the heat of the day made it too hot to work. We spent the middle of each day in Menzies having lunch, reading or sleeping, then we returned to the lake at about 4pm and worked until dark. Everyone had to wear sun-protective clothing, and the repeated application of sunscreen became a ritual. One day I took the morning bus with the volunteers. The initial boisterous jokes, camaraderie, and betting on the time the journey would take (to the second) gave way to the silence of anticipation and sunscreen application. It was hard work.

The third day we were beset by a television crew from the Australian Broadcasting Commission, and Antony and I did not leave the shore until 11am, by which time it was very hot. After about one and a half hours of crunching over the blistering surface, Antony admitted that perhaps it might not have been such a good idea. It was reading 48 °C+ on the digital thermometer. We headed back to shore, Antony's long strides being slowed by the heat and fatigue.

Opposite: Survey flag and marker indicating Insider number and orientation
Following pages: Map showing the planned locations of the Insiders

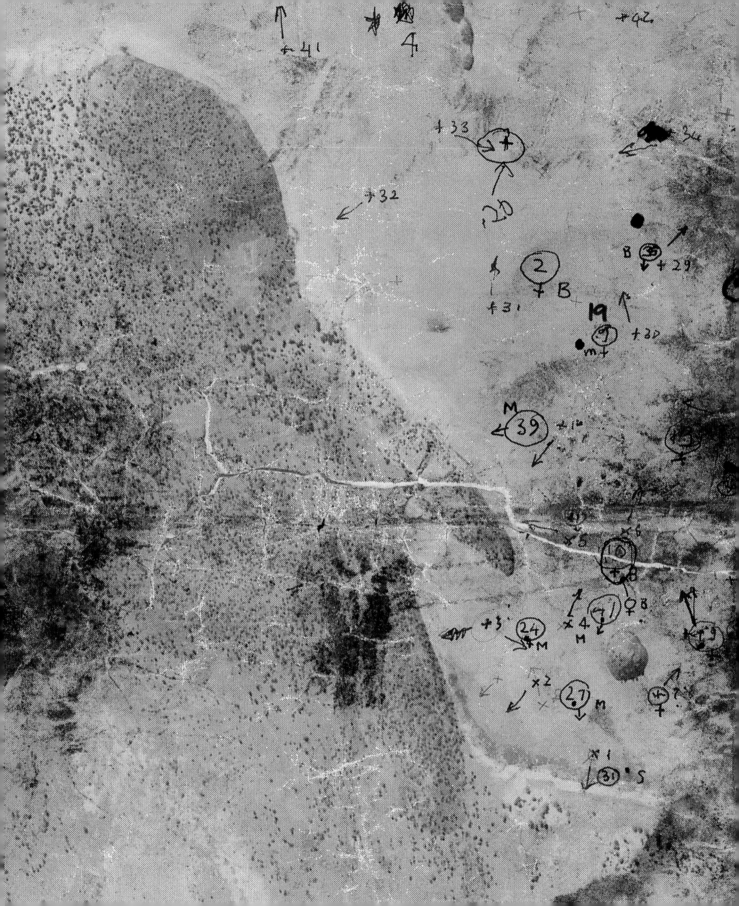

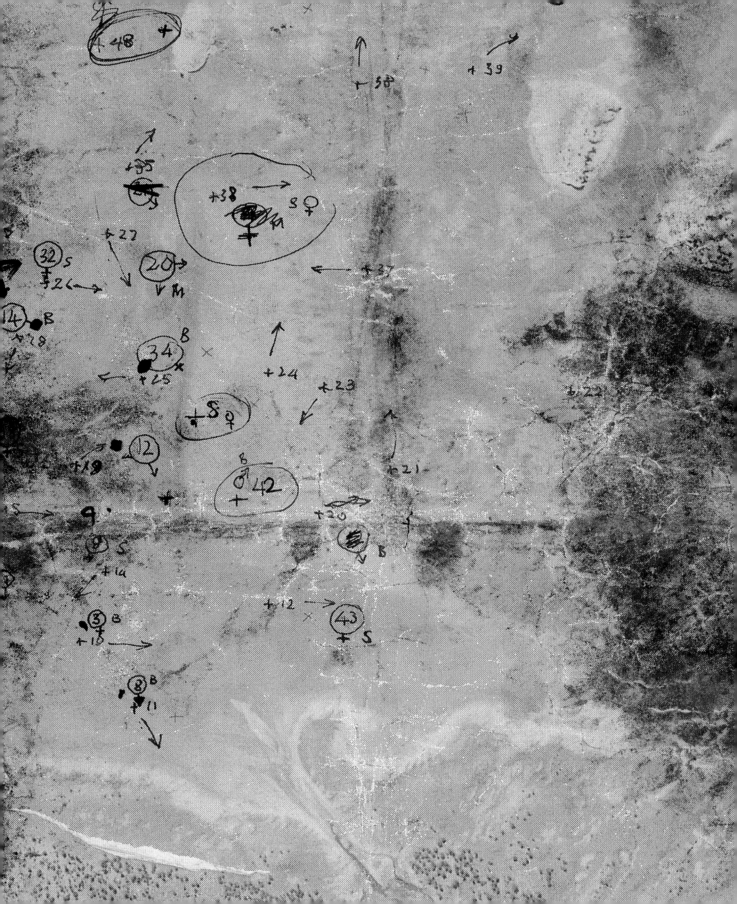

JOB No:	NAME # 1			NAME # 2
082621	27 RICHARD GRAHAM	75	5	TIFFANY PIERCE
083090	12 ALAN HENDERSON	71	8	BRETT KUSIMSKI
083091	22 GUS MILLER	83	21	IAN TUCKER
083271	36 KIETH MADDER	73	43	KEVIN CORBETT
083272	9 JASMINE DOBBIE	29	13	VASHTI SAMBO
083562	28 CAMILLE JOHNSTON	38	4	JENNIFER REED
083565	50 CHRISIEE ARNSHAW	53	15	NATASHA JOHNSTON
083640	23 JOSIE WILLIAMS	74	49	GARY TUCKER
083641	25 AILEEN KELLEY	68	42	ANDREW HOWSE
083801	35 ASHLEY DEPREZER	83	41	PHILIP PARKER
083802	31 JAYDON JOHNSON	TOTAL 140 kg	29	CHAD WICK
083836	20 MATT DYSON	86	48	DARREL ELDRIDGE
083837	37 JEANETTE DOBBIE	28	40	BOB EARNSHAW
083937	7 JANETTE HENDERSON	47	38	KELLIE TUCKER
083938	14 CHRIS DEAVIN	82	26	RACHEAL McCARLIFF
084418	30 JILL DWYER	54	32	KIRA SHEPARD
084144	16 NATHAN COEBERT	24	47	KASHIN ROSS
084220	45 JOHN FINLAYSON	63	44	JOHN REED
084501	39 ROBERT MONEY	108	24 LORRAINE WILLIAMS
084520	17 KAILY TUCKER	109	1	ANTEA JOHNSTON
084542	6 DANIELLE BRENNAN	23	11	LOUISE JOHNSTON
084564	10 JOAN TUCKER	74	18	SIMON JONES
084612	46 ALANA CAMERON	65	24	TRACEY MILNER
084623	33 KATHY FINLAYSON	62	2	JAN MAZZA
084624	3 ESTELLE BLIZZARD	74	9	DEANNE BLIZZARD

Above: Antony Gormley and Finn Pedersen plotting locations for the Insiders

Antony and volunteer Geoff Overheu directing the installation from Snake Hill

Two volunteers taking an Insider to its location

As we approached the shore, Antony said he felt tightness in his chest and his legs had started to cramp — an indication of heat stroke. When we finally sank to our knees below the mulga trees, Todd poured a can of blissfully tepid water over our coddled heads.

In the afternoon the heat was extreme, but as the sun dropped behind Snake Hill and the sky lit up, the lake transformed from glacier-white to deep glowing blue, and the stillness allowed you hear the blood rushing through your veins. At night we recounted stories of lost location flags and salt crystals. One team had reached an especially boggy part on the eastern side of the lake, which we called 'the Somme' (the other was 'Stalingrad' to the north), where the team sank up to their knees in the mud, losing their grip on the Insider. Rather than let it fall in the brown mud, Rob said, 'Lay it on me', and he became a temporary bed for the figure while the team mustered themselves.

On the night of the fifth day we installed the final ring of outer pieces and felt a sense of jubilation. Then, from somewhere towards the setting sun, the sound of bells rang out and we were treated to a sound performance piece by the artist David Jones. The lake resonated like a sounding board — the noise was omnidirectional from where I stood, three and half kilometres offshore. The most distant figure was of a small child beneath an indigo sky. Nearby, lying on the lake, one of the volunteers proposed marriage to his girlfriend. She accepted.

**Inside Australia - An installation
by Antony Gormley**

Presented by the Perth International Arts Festival

Please read carefully for SAFETY ADVICE

• Take at least 5 litres of water per person when walking
  on the lake.
• Wear appropriate sun protection, hat, sunglasses and
  long sleeves is recommended. Be aware that the surface
  of the lake reflects the suns rays. Apply plenty of
  sunscreen at regular intervals. SPF 30+ is recommended.
• Recommended viewing times are in the early morning
  or late afternoon. Allow at least two hours to walk
  around the installation.
• Please view the work in a minimum party of two.
• Please sign the visitors book at Caltex Menzies
  when leaving.
• The lake may be wet and unstable underfoot.
  Wear appropriate footwear.
• DO NOT DRIVE ON THE LAKE.
• Please follow the walking trail from here.
• The mounds and islands have loose rocks on the surface.
  Take care.
• Please take all rubbish away with you.
• Observe all local laws on fire safety - No open fires.
• For advice on camping please enquire at Caltex Menzies.
• Souvenir catalogue and other information is available at
  Caltex Menzies.

For information in Perth contact:
Perth International Arts Festival on
(08) 9380 2000
www.perthfestival.com.au

—Lorraine Williams

Estelle Blizzard

Estelle Blizzard

Darrell Eldridge

Anthea Johnston

Ross Cashin

This page and overleaf: Lorraine Williams

Jayden Johnston

Anthea Johnston with Louise Johnston in background

Robert Earnshaw

Danielle Brennan

Anthea Johnston

Richard Graham

Keith Mader

This page and overleaf: Alana Cameron

Inside Antony Gormley
Anthony Bond

The work of Antony Gormley provides us with important insights into some of the most compelling and radical changes that have occurred in modern sculpture, and even into major changes in the way we think of representation in art. Artists such as Antony have quietly shifted the emphasis away from making images of things in the world towards generating experiences of their presence. These experiences may or may not involve images of the things themselves and may simply provide us with a trace or residue of the thing. Minimalism may have provided a conceptual platform for the idea of material that creates its own presence, however a younger generation have turned Minimalism's literalism upside down by mining this presence for its affective and metaphorical potential.

Two outstanding effects of this shift that further undermine the nature of autonomy of the art work are the incorporation of site into the material meaning of the work and openness between the art work and its active beholder. While modern market conditions might seem to demand portable and self-sufficient objects, many artists working with three dimensions have perversely moved in the opposite direction towards site-specificity.

The other important shift has been away from completely autonomous art objects whose meaning is supposedly inherent in their form, and therefore closed to continuing imaginative work, towards an art that finds its completion in the experiencing mind and body of the viewer. The work of Antony Gormley dramatically embodies these changes. In 1980, he made two works that

importantly marked out a way of thinking about the body in art: not looking at a body but inhabiting the space of the body; not so much representation *of* but affinity *with* the body.

The first of the works, *Room*, was a temporary architectural installation that was also a trace of corporeal absence. Gormley systematically cut his entire bodily coating, from the soles of his shoes, socks and trousers to his shirt and pullover, into thin strips. By knotting these strips together, he made one length that he then wound around four posts to create the space of a room. The body had been texturally expanded to become the room; to enter it would be to enter the space of the artist's body in a disturbingly intimate way. The absence of a door, however, ensured that this remained an imaginary occupation. It is not unusual for clothing to invite imaginary disclosure, just as it patently conceals, but perhaps here it is more a question of finding empathy with the body of another because it is a space or absence rather than a presence. We imaginatively project ourselves into the space rather than look for the absent artist; we might wonder what it would feel like to be in a room that was determined by the shell of another body? We traditionally think of architecture as clothing the body, and classical architecture is suitably predicated on the proportions of the body. When we enter such a building we feel at home, or at least we feel that the space of the building acknowledges us, while we are able to empathize with the prior occupation of others. With *Room*, Gormley announced his interest in exploring the nuances of meaning woven into these relationships.

Bed was an equally intimate and performative work. Gormley made two piles of bread the size of a double bed and proceeded to eat the volume of his own body 'out of the bread', thereby making the negative mould of his own body. In creating the image of his body, he actually consumed himself; communing with his image, he hid himself within himself. It is difficult to stand in front of this piece and not imagine the inside of a body and to think about the experience of eating your own volume of sliced bread. Once again Gormley is inviting empathy between the viewer's body and that of another through the traces of a process. This is not about the image so much as imagining the feeling of being a body. He is finding ways to bypass the representation of the body in favour of something more directly felt.

Gormley's preoccupation with corporeality dates back to the days when he was a student of anthropology and took a unit of art history, choosing the task of piecing together for the first time just how Stanley Spencer's 'Church House' would have looked had Spencer kept all the work together and succeeded in building the architecture to house it. It had been Spencer's dream to build a church based on the plan of the village of Cookham, where he grew up and where he ended up painting so much of his later work. This spiritual space was to have been modelled on community life, where the sacred rooms also reflected daily routines and where the bodily sacrament of sex sat alongside the transcendental sacrament of Holy Communion. Eating the body of Christ is to be filled with the spirit; in this sacrament the body is both actual flesh and a spiritual sign. The spiritual moment is symbolized by the most carnal act. When we commune with God by eating his son, we participate through a literal enactment, an extreme act of empathy – hence why it is called communion. And therein lies a

connection with the way Gormley's art works. His sculpture is not representational, or at least it is not to be read as mimetic. It is providing the house or space for an act of communion.

British art historian Stephen Bann has spoken about some recent sculpture, including Gormley's lead body casings, as participating in a kind of 'ontological communion'. He has taken Hans-Georg Gadamer's phrase out of the context of the religious icon and applied it to sculpture that seems to work as a trace or as an absence that excites our empathetic bodily response. Gadamer's original point was that the religious icon was the exemplary image in painting because, by definition, it could not be a mimetic representation (seraphim do not sit for their portraits). There must therefore be some other relation between image and its object, which he described as ontological communion.

It was a small move from the impression of the body in *Bed*, which took the form of a two-piece mould, to subsequent works in which lead was hammered over a cast of the artist's body to create a hollow shell. It is perhaps these works that most obviously reflect Bann's idea. Gormley has jokingly referred to these lead figures as 'Gormley perdu', a reference to the 'lost wax' casting technique. There is an existential edge to this joke, however, because we are only ever given the trace or the evidence of the artist's passing perhaps as the result of some kind of transmutation, as if these cases were discarded shells like those of insect pupae.

From the beginning, Gormley had these works photographed in the landscape and sought opportunities to have them permanently located where they could be understood in relation to specific architecture or the land. This is no mere romantic impulse but comes close to the core of the work. He has made use of the horizon in several works, including *Land Sea and Air* (1982) and *Another Place* (1997), where the figures are set against the sea and sky, while *The Angel of the*

Page from an undated sketchbook

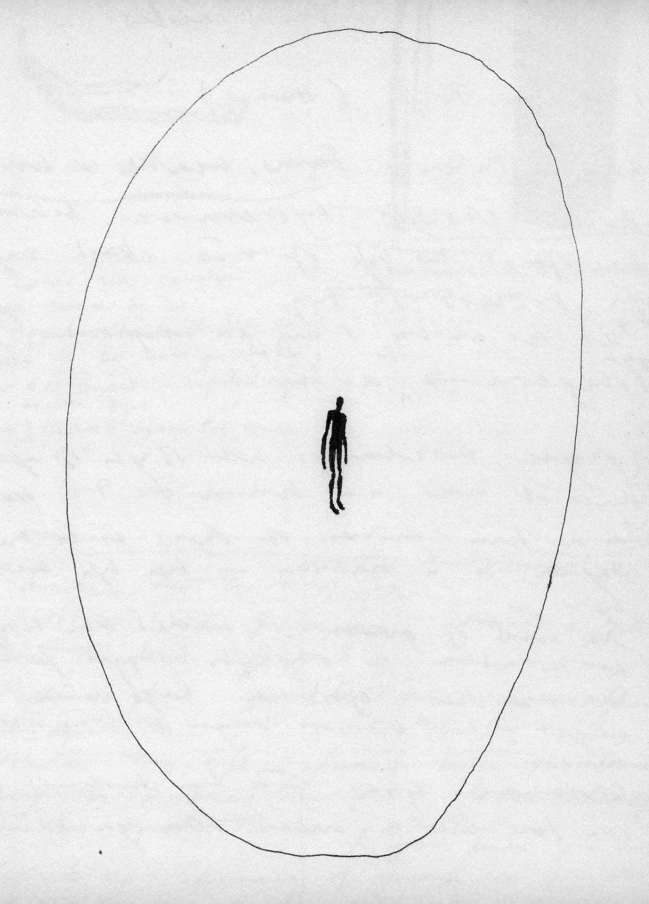

North (1995–8) towers into the sky like a celestial messenger. I do not think this is an accident; these figures are indications of being in the world at the brink of the void. They convey the feeling of sites where consciousness has risen up out of the Earth, and their absent occupants may be thought of as having moved on like the moth that leaves its chrysalis and flies into the sky.

The body and the landscape are intimately bound together, even though modern man lives in a totally fabricated environment – he needs the view from the window into a sense of space. In the end it is always the land that supports life, and it is to the land that the body returns when consciousness passes on. It is an important part of Gormley's project to find ways of placing his figures in the natural or built world so that they draw strength from the nature and spirit of the site while reciprocally lending the place a new kind of significance. It could be argued that this has always been an important element in sculpture, but it has become more expressly stated by artists working with site-specificity, particularly within the landscape since the 1960s and 70s.

In 1977, Walter De Maria created his celebrated *Lightning Field* at Quemado, New Mexico. He installed four hundred highly polished stainless-steel rods in a grid one mile long and one kilometre wide. This field of conducting rods attracts electrical activity to produce a spectacular field of lightning. It is one of the best-known public art works in the modern world and is visited by thousands of people who have probably never heard of Minimalism, conceptual art or land art as such. This popularity attests to the power that art can harness when it reveals natural forces and space, imaginatively connecting both bodily and spiritual feeling.

In the same year, at Documenta VI in Kassel, Germany, De Maria installed another more discreet work, but one that nonetheless focuses an enormous amount of energy, *Vertical earth kilometre*. He sunk a kilometre of brass rod down into the Earth as a vertical column. All that can be seen on the surface is a plaque with the top face of the rod showing. Standing there, knowing that this conducting rod is pointing down to the centre of the Earth below our feet, creates a tangible intensity. Joseph Beuys wore iron shoes when he wanted to be connected to the energy of the planet, with felt soles to insulate himself; one of each set up a flow of energy within his own body. Just imagine how much more energy is physically and metaphorically stored up in this kilometre of sunken metal.

De Maria's work introduces the question of what we need to know in order to fully appreciate the effects of an art work. We tend to think that an exemplary work reveals itself to the senses and thus to the intellect with no external references; however this is not quite how experience ever happens. Antony Gormley wants his figures to be completely self-sufficient, which in a way they are; and yet there is an extraordinary history of ideas and associations with any site in the real world, let alone the symbolic association with gesture that makes the works instantly partake in a web of ideas that enrich our experience the more we discover them.

Richard Serra may come as close as any artist to inducing pure unmediated sensation. The way he sometimes concentrates energy through the simple presence of massive slabs of steel. Twenty tons of steel hammered into a cube of approximately one metre in size not only reveals the once fluid state of the metal and the vast force of the industrial hammer that beats it into shape, but also creates such a density of matter that its magnetic field makes the hairs on your neck tingle and stand on end. To walk inside one of Serra's spiral steel-plate structures is to experience immense spatial compression and disorientation. It produces an effect that is similar to the almost unbearable physical thrill a child experiences beside the thundering immensity of a steam engine.

157

Opposite: Sketch drawn during the Lake Ballard project, 2002
Following pages: Early proposal, in which explosives would blast away craters from the lake's surface and sculptures would be made from the metals extracted from the material, 2001

Already, of course, my description makes associations with lived experience, and this is the dilemma for the purist of sensation.

Converting the viewer into an actor is another important aspect of this kind of sculpture. This performative aspect of Minimalism was first articulated by Michael Fried in his 1967 essay 'Art and Objecthood' as a negative critique of its theatricality, but writers such as Rosalind Krauss and Hal Foster later turned around his arguments. Foster's article 'The Crux of Minimalism' provides the clearest statement of the presentness of the object and the value of an art that engages the viewer's presence in its completion. The works of Serra and De Maria are not just for looking at but need to be engaged with somatically and imaginatively. But it is not always necessary for the art work to be monumental to achieve this sense of bodily engagement. Carl Andre has made a series of metal-plate compositions, including *Venus forge* (1980) at Tate Modern, where different metals are arranged in squares of various dimensions. These are laid on the floor with the expectation that the viewer will walk over them. There is of course an immense inhibition that most of us feel at walking on an art work. After all, there are many floor-based installations that are destroyed by being walked on or even near. The tension of walking or not walking is a strong element in determining the viewer's concrete presence in the space and their connection with the work.

As a contrast with Andre's metal plates, we might consider an installation at the Stephen Friedman Gallery in London, *Untitled* (1999) by Rivane Neuenschwander. Onto the parquet floor of the gallery the artist had meticulously sprinkled thin lines of white marble powder to cover exactly the cracks between the wooden blocks. This fine and labour-intensive installation covered the entire floor except for a narrow passage around the outside edges of the room framing the work. Walking around the floor drawing, one becomes intensely aware of the fragility of the material, a misplaced footstep – or for that matter a sneeze – would prove fatal for the whole installation. Neuenschwander's fragile sensibility confers great responsibility onto the viewer, underlining their commitment to the work. Anne Hamilton is another installation artist who often works with the floor, strewing it with material that rustles or crackles underfoot. Works by these artists make the viewer very conscious of their own presence as a part of the installation and of their potentially destructive power or complicity in the realization of the event that their presence initiates, as if with every viewer the work is remade. Such works deliberately highlight the presence of the viewer and their self-consciousness of being with the work. It is an installational equivalent of Jasper John's strategy with his number paintings. The heavily crusted impasto numbers in encaustic and metallic paint suggest some monumental purpose or content, yet on close inspection they prove to be devoid of any logical significance; they are just motifs. Deprived of any reading, the viewer is thrown back into awareness of 'the process of their looking', as Australian artist and theorist Ian Burn put it, 'looking at seeing not reading'.

This history of presence has largely been non-figurative, with the viewer providing the living animation to it. The background to this has been the relative difficulty of a realist treatment of the body in twentieth-century art. As Modernism unpicked the conventional purposes and means of visual representation, the body underwent all kinds of fragmentation, such as distortion in the name of expressivity or the analysis of representational means as in Cubism. In the wake of this dismantling of appearance, abstraction seemed for a while the only way to deal with the metaphysics of presence, with the exception of Surrealism, which dealt more in dreams than in the real; but it was Surrealism and Dada that introduced traces of real life in the form of found objects, preparing the way for Minimalism and subsequent artistic strategies.

A page from a sketchbook, *c.* 1998

Gormley was one of the first artists to return successfully to the body in sculpture. All non-photographic representations of the body after Modernism are problematic; sculpture, however, is more difficult than painting as it occupies real space with its material presence. Sculptures are objects in the world as well as indicating some other, not present thing. The way forward as shown by the Minimalists was to converge the sign and the referent, thereby eliminating this awkward duality. But the price they paid was the metaphorical dimension of art that is its most enduring instrument.

Gormley's success is in large part due to his intuitive explorations of the kind of presence initiated through Minimalism that bypasses the nature of representation, while recapturing the possibility of metaphysical references to culture, and above all to the experience of the body. His works function as trace and invocation of the body, and not necessarily as its likeness. The body is not distorted here except as a function of the process of its production. The lead casings paradoxically gain their auratic quality through the absence that the casings signal, not through likeness of that which in fact they obscure – that is, the absent body over which they were formed.

Gormley always acknowledges the history and atmosphere of the site where he is working. *Sound II* (1986), for example, is installed in the crypt of Winchester Cathedral. The lead figure stands in water since the crypt is more often than not flooded. It appears with head bowed, absorbed in a pool of water held in its cupped hands. It immediately brings to mind the magical pool in which the seer can travel over distance and time. In 1997, Gormley installed *Another Place* consisting of one hundred cast-iron standing figures in the shallow tidal flats near Klugelbake on the German coast. These figures all face out to sea. They are not walking out to sea, just standing as sentinels; not holding back the tide but witnessing its advance and retreat. Their eyes are fixed on the horizon, that boundary between the known world and what lies beyond the limit of human sensibility at the meeting of sea and sky. The figures seem to be contemplating their place in the world between matter and mind, here at the edge of the world just like Caspar David Friedrich's *Monk by the Sea* (c. 1809).

It was to the land that Gormley turned when in 1989 he came to Sydney to install *A field for the Art Gallery of NSW* at the Gallery and to locate a reciprocal work in the desert, *A room for the great Australian desert*. He requested a site with 360 degrees of uninterrupted flat horizon and red dust underfoot. I located a spot where I knew that the clay pans were extensive and the horizon was terrifyingly flat and low. Standing up there, you are the highest object this side of the horizon. It is a vertiginous experience, as if you could fall from the spinning globe. It was while camping out here that Gormley talked to me about Heidegger and the phenomenological problem of consciousness that rests so lightly upon the material world from which it has arisen and yet is always constructed as its Other. There could be no more dramatic and appropriate place for such speculations and for an art work that embodies them.

The work Gormley made for the Gallery was a field of 1,100 little clay figures made from the red bull dust of the centre of Australia. The figures were arranged in two hemispheres mimicking the plan of the brain, with a pathway down the middle to a central lobe where you stand. From this vantage point you become aware that all the figures have eyes focused directly on you. I immediately responded to this mass gaze with guilt, felt on behalf of mankind that has so badly bruised the land out of which it arose. Others claim to feel godlike. Perhaps both feelings are appropriate; to judge is to be judged, after all.

Back in the desert, Gormley positioned a concrete body housing. It was designed to house exactly his own body within its cubic form. The

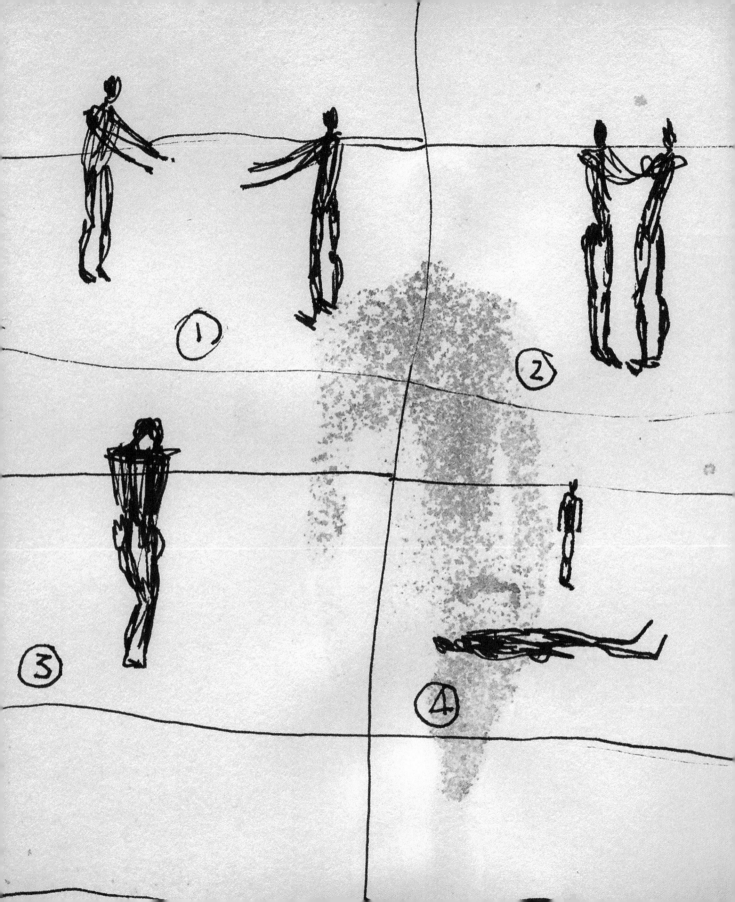

figure has a powerful presence in the land even though there is no one to see it. The station manager tells me he has seen it from the air but not visited the site. What Gormley anticipates is that creatures of the desert, spiders, crickets and lizards will have reanimated the hollow form. He has made a number of these architectural suits since then, some of them designed to fit precisely the individual measurements of members of a community. With this and other works like it, Gormley has shifted from the singularity of the artist's figure to a position that bears witness to a collective body.

When camping out in the desert, one often comes across places that feel comfortable and welcoming. This is not to do with any known human history and only in part due to topographical and climatic features. An outcrop of rock can have caves on either side and they may be completely different in atmosphere. One side may even be rather terrifying with an atmosphere of foreboding, while a few metres away an overhang beckons you inside and provides comfort for the night's sleep. The extraordinary thing about the 'good' cave is that it always has evidence of multiple occupations of thousands of years of cricket and bat droppings, kangaroo and other marsupial traces that are completely missing from the 'bad' cave. The Chinese have codified something of this mystery in Feng Shui, but all sentient beings seem to have intuitive responses to particular spaces. I suppose one might measure the success of Gormley's A room for the great Australian desert by the number of insects that have chosen to animate its interior.

There are undoubtedly many logical factors involved in this history of choices that also explain the atmosphere of the space. The body responds very strongly to space and atmosphere and this is a crucial component in the most interesting recent sculpture, just as it has been in the siting of sacred monuments, such as the standing stones of the

British Isles or, for that matter, the choice of a particular tree or rock for a Shona tree shrine in East Africa and of trees that are sacred to particular Aboriginal communities. It may also be possible, however, to generate the energy required to create such a place through sheer mass or through focus of energy, as for example with Walter De Maria and Richard Serra.

Inside Australia is part of a series of works by Gormley that seek to decentre the focus of energy from the artist as subject, or even as model for a figure, and to engage in a more communal and collaborative project. This series can be thought of as having its origins in the groupings of body casings, although they were always traces of the artist in various manifestations or stages of the unfolding drama. It was probably with the various Field works that the break came. Not only did the figures become ideations rather than traces of the artist's own body, but their forms were roughly made in response to the hands of the people who helped make them and thus form traces of these others. These works were also decidedly masses of figures and not individual markers of space. The romantic figure on the seashore was replaced by the masses that surge up from the earth to populate the world. Gormley badly wants to take his place in this throng and help to give it a voice.

Since then, other bodies have played an important role, even in the more architectural pieces such as Allotment (1996), where the cubic casings were not based on his own body but on the measurements of members of a local community who volunteered to take part. These works depend on a rigorous mathematical extension of the body from the organic to the cubic, while other works make the figure into the absent core of an apparently non-human form.

The Insiders seem to reverse the concept of a body casing that contains a void indicating its absence. The process is similar, however, and depends equally on a direct relation between the

165

body and a system of measurement. It is this systematic dependence on tracing the real that determines the authenticity of the work and continues to convey an uncanny sense of the body's presence. The first of Gormley's Insiders was produced using a mechanical system of templates to reduce the mould of the body to thirty per cent of its original mass. While this process changes its appearance and form, even making it strange, it is a rigorous procedure rather than an expressive gesture. Our affective reaction is to the thing itself as a corporeal response to experiencing the body's exterior being interiorized.

Subsequently, Gormley adopted computer scanning techniques to reduce the mass of the body parts while retaining the vertical dimensions and the width of the hips and shoulders. The tips of breasts and penises also seem to retain their distance from the core (spine?), thereby forming elongated shapes in the same way that the limbs are distorted. This reduction has nothing skeletal about it, nothing literal in fact since the condensed forms bear no visual relation to the superficial appearance of the body's form. In spite of this, they suggest a core feeling of the body in question; they excite the sensation of internal strength, a secret space to which the individual might withdraw; and they also capture the characteristic movement of individual bodies. They are precise portraits of real individuals and, despite the extreme contraction of the forms, the sitters seem to be able to recognize themselves.

Inside Australia employs this computerized technique of reduction, but of equal artistic importance is Gormley's commitment to working with a community and with a specific place. Lake Ballard is a remote location and one with a very particular history that is described elsewhere in this book. Aboriginal occupation has been interrupted by pastoralism, and then displaced by goldmining. Today the mines still exist but the once-thriving towns have shrunk to tiny communities of casual

workers and there is little work for the remaining Aboriginal people. The goldfields are a wild place to visit. Vast flat expanses of semi-desert have been denuded of indigenous plants and wildlife by the introduction of imported livestock. Occasional 'breakaway' ridges of sandstone, ironstone and tough stunted bushes that grow in the red dust relieve the flatness. Quartz chips that glow in the moonlight punctuate the redness, and occasional reefs of mica shimmer like broken glass. There are itinerant prospectors, and occasional casual employment brings strangers from far away. Pastoral use has shrunk to a fraction of its original strength; stations are isolated and often run by one manager and his family – if he is lucky enough to have one. This is a harsh climate and territorial rights are regularly enforced at gunpoint.

This is the unlikely place that Gormley came to make friends and to produce a portrait of the community that would put the people back in the landscape. It might be that this work could be thought of as a kind of restitution: it brings all sections of this community together in a common project, placing them back into the landscape together and eliminating the outward signs of difference while maintaining their individuality. Gormley successfully negotiated the collaboration of potentially unsympathetic inhabitants of the area, and in the process brought disparate people together. It is an attractive possibility to think of art as healing, and yet there is something melancholic, even lost about the figures, and nothing is ever that simple when you engage real histories and real places. It may be best to describe the experience of visiting the site, since an important part of this work is the difficult journey we must make to find it, the impact on us of that journey, the sense of discovery when we arrive, the people we meet and of course the extraordinary feeling of the space itself.

Menzies is the nearest town to Lake Ballard, 150 kilometres north of Kalgoorlie, which is the biggest centre in the goldfields and has an airport

166

something like — another place but with
the insides — could they be made of
gold? — just 3 of them — pure
gold — or is the symmetrism too heavy
— perhaps Molibdenum — or Zenobium —
something recent on the periodic table —
and if it was radioactive enough
no-one would be able to come near
they could hear about it . . . . .

Instrumentation.
_____

Antennae.
make cases for everyone
make ones for everyone

with regular commercial flights. Kalgoorlie still has a frontier feel to it and a few minutes drive out of the centre the bush very quickly takes over. There are occasional signs for goldmines by the road and some of these mines are visible as great slag heaps and tangles of corrugated iron buildings. Menzies would be easy to miss; there are only a few buildings left, spread out amongst the gritty waste. The main street is also the highway north, and this short street retains a dim trace of past glory. The Menzies hotel and the garage are the two remaining businesses, while over the road are the modest but charmingly historic council buildings. Looking at the pub it is possible to see how it has seen greater days. Menzies was once home to thousands of people with quick money to spend; today you are lucky to see five or six in a day.

When I arrived at the hotel, the only place to stay in town, there were about that number of people in the bar. Some of them had come in from outstations and decided to stay the night after a few beers, and others were locals. Three of them were Aboriginals: one ran the local community centre, another drove the grader for council, and I never quite worked out what the third did, but it was getting late.

I did not disclose my interest in Gormley but began a casual conversation about the sculpture out on the lake. Not only were all of them, including Keith our host, keen to talk, they were all adamant that the work had to stay there. When I asked what people made of it, they said that the longer it stayed the more people would identify with it and come to have their own stories about it. They were also proud that the number of visitors to the town had risen from a handful in a week to as many as ten people in a day at weekends. Many of the visitors had come from Europe and, of course, all had stayed at the hotel. In spite of the large building and the small number of people staying there, our accommodation was in containerized temporary cells out the back near a

mobile ablutions block. It must have been an interesting experience for our foreign visitors.

I set out for the site at 5.30am in order to catch the sunrise, which is Gormley's preferred viewing time. It is a forty-minute drive in daylight, but missing the large grey kangaroos that bolted across the road in front of us in the dark made it more like an hour. There is a designated parking area a little distance away from the site itself – which is a very good idea, as cars parked along the lakeshore would break the spell. I was relieved to see no one else had made it at this early hour because I had a romantic desire to be alone at this first encounter. There is a sign at the car park advising that we take at least five litres of water with us, always wear a hat and never venture out alone – too late for me now! It is necessary to approach the lake on foot because this prepares you for the scale of humanity in relation to the great outback. In my case it also involved an encounter with one of the giant goannas that frequent this prehistoric landscape.

Lake Ballard first appears as you climb a shallow rise. It is a large expanse of white saltpan with a small conical hill named Snake Hill at the centre of the vista. Gormley has ensured us a perfect approach to the site. From a few hundred metres away, you can already detect one of the figures against the whiteness near the hill. As you approach the edge of the lake itself, you begin to see the rest of the sculptures stretching out as far as the eye can see. Some hundred to two hundred metres or more separates them from each other, but there is no obvious pattern to their spacing. Unlike the coastal works in Europe, these figures are not all gazing out into the lake but stand about randomly disposed. In the early light of day, their shadows stretch out for ever. The surface of the lake reflected the colours of the sky, turning shades of pink and Parma violet. This effect was enhanced because it had rained recently and the lake was temporarily flooded.

169

Opposite and following pages: Early ideas for the Lake Ballard project, 2001

172

While the waters had thankfully retreated enough to allow me to walk out on the reforming salt crust, half a kilometre out there was a skin of water possibly one or two millimetres thick covering the salt and shimmering brilliantly in the raking dawn light. Unfortunately, however, it did not permit me to walk all the way out to the furthest figures seven kilometres away.

From a distance, the figures seem very natural, like real people in the landscape. It is possible to recognize a certain characteristic pose for each individual. You read the pose rather than the detail of the figure and it is only as you approach that the formal reduction of the figures becomes apparent. The effect of their reduction produces a very strange sensation; there is something very naked about them. They have an uncanny presence, something unhuman, and yet they carry with them something intensely personal to the 'sitter'. While Giacometti's figures are monumental and a little impersonal, reflecting the vision of the artist rather than the original model, these sculptures are strangely vulnerable and are not distanced by the artist's gesture. Giacometti's reduction of the figure to a slender linear form is expressive of the artist's vision and uses no systematic proportional system. The surfaces are very rough, revealing the soft clay and the hand of the artist who reduces the figure to this strip of flayed flesh. By contrast, Gormley's figures have smooth surfaces articulated only by the procedures of mechanical reduction so that they have a direct relationship to the real figure while not mimicking its appearance. In this way, they are like the lead figure casings – they are a real trace of the thing itself and not a contrived or expressive manipulation of nature.

The two optimum viewing moments are dawn and dusk, when the light quality transforms the figures. The steel figures seem black against the salt during the burning light of midday but change to reflect the sunset and sunrise, almost seeming to radiate a red or purple glow at these times.

I returned before dusk to find a number of people had gathered there in small groups, no more than two or three together, spread out over the lake, which had dried significantly since morning. The temperature had risen to the upper 40s by the time I left and must have been fierce all day. Snake Hill provides a magnificent elevated view over the landscape and from there you can see the entire lake and appreciate the full extent of the installation. From a distance, it was sometimes hard to distinguish the living from the Insiders. It seemed to me as if all of us living and otherwise sharing this space were lost in our own thoughts.

This installation may be the portrait of a community in its place but it has a universal dimension as well. The experience of being among these figures in the lake engages our own sense of scale in the land. It bridges the gap between the conscious mind of the human as possessor and master of the world with a truer and more intuitive feeling of being at one with it. This is a grand scenario, and yet the impact of the landscape is not that of the awesome sublime. In spite of the harshness, the heat, the blinding light of midday and the vast void of the salt lake, Gormley brings us to a momentary experience of belonging, not to the goldfields but to the Earth. We stand not so much on the brink of the void but at the point of absorption, where consciousness merges into material, a word that has *mater* (mother) as its root. The salt of the lake, residue of the recycling waters, is a powerful reminder of our own bodily composition, as was evidenced by a crust of salt that had formed itself over my brow.

Opposite: A page from a sketchbook, c. 1998
Following pages: Early distribution idea for the Insiders, 2001

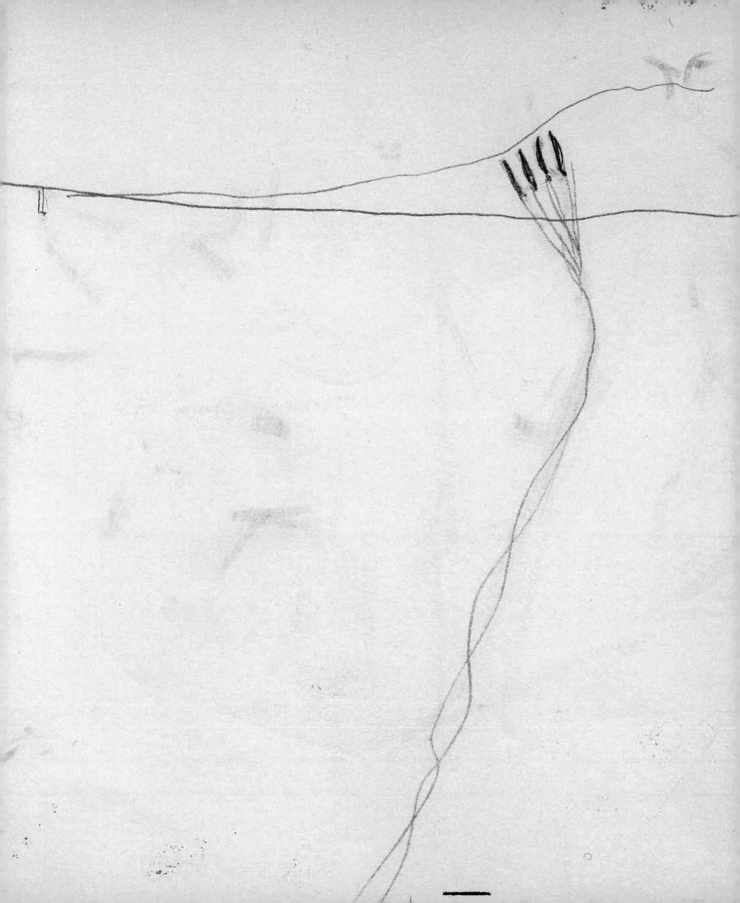

Notes on the Project

Site information
- Menzies is 132 km north of Kalgoorlie and 729 km east of Perth in Western Australia; Lake Ballard is approximately 55 km from Menzies.
- The site's coordinates are 29° 26' latitude and 120° 36' longitude.
- The lake is estimated to be one million years old.
- Average annual rainfall is 251.2 mm.
- Temperatures range from –4.8 °C to 46.2 °C.
- The lake surface is a silty clay layer on top of gypsum gravel.
- Snake Hill, the conical hill in the middle of the lake, is an ironstone intrusion.
- The vegetation of the area is samphire bush, eucalypt, mulga scrub, wattle woodlands and scattered sandelwood trees.
- Lake Ballard is a breeding ground for banded stilts, red-capped plovers, red-necked avocets, grey teal and the hooded plover.
- Beneath the crust of the lake, the mud supports brine shrimp and micro-organisms.
- The work covers approximately ten square kilometres.

The scanning process
- Software design and scanning operation was by headus (metamorphosis) in Perth.
- 131 people were scanned in Menzies and in Perth.
- Each scan took seventeen seconds and created half a million digital coordinates.
- Each person's body volume was reduced by two thirds in a process called 'gormleyization'.
- An online virtual workshop was set up allowing workers on the project to access the material from around the world.

The lost foam process
- Digital files of the 'gormleyized' scans were sent from Perth to a polystyrene mill in Sydney.
- Polystyrene patterns were milled with a cadcam system directly from the digital file.
- The patterns were sent back to the VEEM Foundry in Perth for individual assembly.
- It took three hours to assemble each polystyrene figure.
- The polystyrene figures were then encased in a sand mould.

Casting the Insiders
- Metal was poured through feeders into the sand mould at 1555 °C.
- The polystyrene figures were burned away as the metal replaced it – a process that took one second.
- The molton metal was a stainless-steel alloy: iron 67%, chromium 20%, nickel 11%, molybdenum 2%, and trace elements of vanadium and titanium oxide from Lake Ballard.
- The sculptures were then heat treated at 1050 °C.
- The final colour of the sculptures comes from the carbonization of the surface during the heat treatment.
- The sculptures range in weight from 16 kg to 131 kg.
- Fifteen people in the foundry worked on the project.
- It took approximately forty hours to make each sculpture.

Transport and installation
- The sculptures travelled 780 km from the foundry in Perth to the site on Lake Ballard.
- A team of eighteen volunteers and Perth International Arts Festival staff installed the work over five days.
- Temperatures on the site reached over 48 °C during the installation.

The Insiders
Deanne Blizzard, Estelle Blizzard, Danielle Brennan, Alana Cameron, Ross Cashin, Kevin Corbett, Nathan Corbett, Chris Deavin, Ashley de Prazer, Jasmine Dobbie, Jeanette Dobbie, Jill Dwyer, Matthew Dyson, Christine Earnshaw, Robert Earnshaw, Darrell Eldridge, John Finlayson, Kath Finlayson, Richard Graham, Allan Henderson, Janet Henderson, Andrew Howse, Anthea Johnston, Camille Johnston, Jayden Johnston, Louise Johnston, Natasha Johnston, Simon Jones, Aileen Kelly, Brett Kuzimski, Alison McArdle, Rachel McAuliffe, Keith Mader, Samantha Mazza, Gus Miller, Tracey Milner, Rob Money, Phillip Parker, Tiffany Pierce, Jennifer Reid, John Reid, Vashti Sambo, Kyra Shepherd, Chadwick Tucker, Gary Tucker, Ian Tucker, Joan Tucker, Kaylene Tucker, Kellie Tucker, Josie Williams, Lorraine Williams

Installation volunteers
Dean Adams, Shaun Atkinson, Michelle Blakeley, Samuel Cheong, Ahrna Edwards, Benjamin Ryan Garwood, Carol Hemund, Rhys Jenkins, George Kailis, Chiew Mei Law, Johnsen Lim, Sally Mason, Rob McLeod, Geoff Overheu, Sam Overheu, Lisa Shine, Daniel Szabo, Patrick Tantra

Perth Festival staff
Sean Doran, Festival Director
Wendy Wise, General Manager
Alison McArdle, Festival Producer
Shelagh Magadza, Project Manager
Drew Dymond, Production Manager
Adam Richards, Technical Coordinator
Finn Pedersen, Installation Manager
Todd Westbrook, Installation Crew
Rupert Sewell, Installation Crew

Thanks to
The Menzies Shire, Menzies Aboriginal Corporation, Goldfields Land and Sea Council, Aubrey Lynch, Paddy Walker, Wangkatha and Wutha peoples, Riverina Station, Professor David Jones, Iredale Pedersen Hook Architects, University of Western Australia Architecture Department and Curtin University Fine Arts Department student volunteers, University of Western Australia Geology Department, VEEM Engineering Group, Arup Geotechnics, headus (metamorphosis), Ashley de Prazer Photography